D1594977

# Carl Nielsen

*by* Jack Lawson

Φ

**'She had been my helper and friend for my whole life; and I can say that without my dear mother,
I would have become nothing ... there will never be another of her character.'**

**Carl Nielsen, to the composer Bror Beckman**

Phaidon Press Limited
Regent's Wharf
All Saints Street
London N1 9PA

First published 1997
© 1997 Phaidon Press Limited

ISBN 0 7148 3507 2

A CIP catalogue record for this book is
available from the British Library

Printed in Singapore

*Frontispiece*, two informal
photographs of the young
Carl Nielsen dating from the
early 1880s

# Contents

# Acknowledgements

A Nielsen biography is so overdue that the publishers, Phaidon Press, must be acknowledged for instigating it. Literary sources are sparse. In September 1994, as work on this book proceeded, the death was announced of Mr Reginald Spink. In 1953 he had published the celebrated translations of Nielsen's own two books – the story of his childhood on Fyn and the collection of essays on musical topics. Ronald Adlem, who became a friend of the composer's younger daughter, and his colleague, Brian Duke, kindly permitted me to use their (as yet unpublished) translation of the 1954 collection of letters and their work in progress on memoirs of Anne Marie Telmányi, the composer's younger daughter. Nielsen's elder daughter, Irmelin, found a fine friend, and the English-speaking world its most influential guide to the symphonies, in the composer Robert Simpson, whose earlier career was as a writer and BBC producer. In 1987 the American pianist and musicologist Mina Miller compiled a helpful bibliography, *Carl Nielsen: A Guide to Research*, and the collection of essays she edited was published in 1994.

From the start of my research in 1989 I was greatly encouraged by the leading authority on Carl Nielsen, Torben Schousboe of the University of Copenhagen, who, during crucial years of Nielsen neglect, was a lone crusader. For his friendship, inspiration and impressive grip on every aspect of Nielsen as both a human being and a creative artist, I am more grateful than I can say. His reference works have been invaluable to all subsequent studies of his remarkable compatriot and kindred spirit. After Copenhagen, the second active centre of Nielsen activity and research is Odense, capital of the island region of Fyn where Nielsen was born and where he lived until he became a student. Here my correspondent is Jørgen Larsen whom I met while he was working on one of his projects for the Carl Nielsen Museum in Odense. In connection with the restoration of the Nielsen childhood cottage, Mr Larsen came up with new information about Nielsen's youth.

Susanne Thorbek of the Royal Library in Copenhagen and Birthe Fraser of the Royal Danish Embassy in London earn my special thanks. David Fanning read the text as it neared completion, and despite his cruel workload as lecturer at Manchester University, critic and writer (lending me his own manuscript-in-progress on Nielsen's fifth symphony) he generously found time to contribute many valuable suggestions. The pianist Peter Seivewright (who has recorded the complete piano works) also made helpful suggestions and together we had as many hours of stimulating discussions as our hectic schedules would allow. Nielsen's complexity is such that I am still not sure we were talking about the same composer! Many other people, too numerous to list, from whose writings and comments I have benefited also merit my thanks, as do the musicians whose fine performances were a powerful source of inspiration to me (of special note is Opera North's sparkling 1990 production of *Maskarade*).

To return full cycle to record my gratitude to Phaidon Press, I wish to acknowledge valued support and advice from editors Norman Lebrecht, Roger Sears, Peter Owens and Ingalo Thomson. My thanks also to the picture researcher Michèle Faram and Hans Dieter Reichert of hdr design.

Jack Lawson
Glasgow, 1997

# Introduction

On 22 September 1931 Carl Nielsen, the grand old man of Danish music, while supervising a dress rehearsal of his comic opera, *Maskarade*, climbed up the ropes backstage at Copenhagen's Theatre Royal. The 66-year-old composer was showing a young stagehand how to unravel tangled scenery. His recently whitened hair and the loss of his boyish looks betrayed the tightening grip of angina pectoris. The strain on his heart after helping the stagehand had been too great and he was accompanied to his home opposite the canal. He did not think it was serious, but on the advice of his son-in-law – a practising doctor – he agreed to go to the municipal hospital. On the bleak evening of 3 October his opera was playing to another full and enthusiastic house. As the character of Corporal Mors entered the stage, his creator drifted into a coma from which he was not to recover.

It was remarkable that Nielsen, in view of his disadvantaged childhood, would become a highly regarded composer of symphonies and dramatic works, although it was clear that he would become some sort of musician. From his childhood in Fyn, sounds and rhythms had represented the poetry of movement and the essence of life for him. His interest in music was encouraged by his parents, in spite of their poverty and their isolation from high culture, and at the age of fourteen he joined a military band in Odense. Only ten years after a photograph of him was taken as a newly-promoted junior corporal in the regimental band, his music-making was to culminate in a remarkable first symphony, followed by compositions which the gentlemen of the Royal Danish Music Conservatoire saw as a real challenge to the music of the nineteenth century.

Nielsen revolutionized the musical world with his musical innovations, primary amongst them his 'progressive tonality'. And when he died in 1931, the compositions of his former teachers, J. P. E. Hartmann and Niels Gade, had begun to sound old-fashioned and a new style of popular Danish song fashioned by Carl Nielsen was on the lips of choirs, congregations, school children and ordinary people in the factories and fields. For better or worse, the style of composition of the generation of Danish composers that followed Nielsen skipped a whole period of musical development – from late-Romantic music directly to the sonorities of the mid twentieth century – because the influence of Carl Nielsen in his native country eclipsed that of contemporary central European figures.

During his lifetime his own countrymen were divided in their praise of his work. Not until midway through his career, in 1911, when he produced two key works (the Third Symphony and the Violin Concerto) did critics and colleagues fully recognize that here was a musical force to be reckoned with. This was twenty years after his First Symphony. In his youth Nielsen had prophetically confided to his diary: 'The artist who is handy with his fists will secure for himself the most lasting posthumous reputation: Beethoven ... Bach, Berlioz ... and similar men have all given their contemporaries a black eye!' To this day the life and music of Carl Nielsen continue to polarize opinion, and the extent of his influence and achievements remains a subject of controversy.

The scope and independence of his aims and methods defy conventional labelling, placing him outside the mainstream as much as did the isolation of Denmark. He was no narrow symphonist, anti-Romantic, modernist or nationalist. Was he a revolutionary or a revisionist? This is a crucial question but something of an enigma. He himself said that revolutions belonged to politics not art, and yet, his music was arguably more modern and experimental than that of his contemporary, the Finnish composer Jean Sibelius, whose work is more the distinguished revision of nineteenth-century masters. Nielsen's music returned to the pristine styles of the sixteenth-century roots of Western music, from which he developed an advanced tonality, counterpoint and rhythm. For Nielsen musical progress meant simplification – the discarding of obsolete and overworked traditions. He expressed negativity and ugliness by means of dissonance and peculiar rhythm but he rarely betrayed despair or resorted to musical 'bad language'.

Nielsen had his complexities, but he was a not complicated man: he was reflective without being either introverted or morose; he was a man of action; individualistic but not eccentric. A man more receptive to the sound of rustling leaves and birdsong than to any academic theories of composition, Nielsen was driven by a healthy vigour – as opposed to any kind of inner turmoil or the need to reject the world – and many who have become familiar with his music testify to its invigorating powers. It grows and promotes growth through the generations, as Goethe said of Mozart's music.

Nielsen the man and Nielsen the artist are two sides of one coin: his life and work cannot be separated even if the autobiographical elements of his music are more concealed than those of many other composers. His outlook was that of *l'art pour l'art*: art as an end in itself. He wrote for posterity, not the critics, although he was greatly encouraged by a receptive audience and a favourable press. The spiritual aspect of life, as he saw it, encompassed all its human, natural and enduring aspects and he chose a musical career because he believed that only music, of all the arts, could directly express these. From the *Little Suite for Strings* (1888) to *Commotio* for organ (1931) one constant theme unites a wide gulf of musical development and style. It is the humanist ideology, or what may be termed as 'the phenomenon of Man'. Nielsen's music grew from behavioural traits he had directly observed, in contrast to the central European soul-searching of many of his contemporaries. He was also often inspired by poems and paintings but not by religious or philosophical systems or works. His music has been described as concerning the life-force. 'Music is life' is his most quoted comment, and its deeper meaning is the central message of this book.

His death in 1931 was keenly felt in his native Denmark, precip-itating a torrent of obituaries, musical analyses and reminiscences by friends and colleagues. Nevertheless, sixty-five years after his death his letters and diaries are yet to be opened to the scholarly world and remain unlisted. Only two full-length biographies, by Torben Meyer and Ludwig Dolleris, published in 1948 and 1949 respectively, have been based on original research. Jørgen I. Jensen's long-awaited book *Carl Nielsen – danskeren* ('Carl Nielsen the Dane') appeared in 1991 as a specialist study of the composer in the context of his Danish culture. All three works are in Danish, but Meyer's text, translated into English, was shoe-horned into an appendix to Robert Simpson's 1952 study of the symphonies. From these works was born the fairy-tale legend of the 'untainted nature boy', the poor farm lad who overcame all obstacles to become his nation's musical grandee.

The primary sources, the recollections of Nielsen's friends and colleagues, critical reviews and even the composer's own writings and notes, are often so ambiguous and contradictory that some perspective is required to grasp the true nature of Carl Nielsen. Only with a full-length biography, not hitherto available in English, can readers catch a glimpse of a forceful, intriguing character brimming with vitality.

I

The cottage where Carl
Nielsen was born in 1865,
represented in an oil painting
by his brother Albert

*If, from a lofty mountain in the middle of Fyn,
we could look down over the whole island,
tracing its outline against the blue sea, we
should make the delightful discovery that Fyn,
viewed this way too, is one of the fairest of lands
... But there is no mountain ... The land of Fyn
never changes; it lies safe and sound where, after
gentle but firm reflection, it resolved to cast
anchor. How quietly and gracefully it slid in
between Jylland and Sjælland!*

Carl Nielsen, *Living Music*, 1925

## A Rural Childhood 1865–79

'The Garden of Denmark' is the nickname often given to Fyn, the smallest of the country's three regions. Its distinctive charms have, inevitably, succumbed to modernization but traditional features have been preserved in the island's many museums. Of these, the Cottage of Hans Christian Andersen in Odense attracts by far the most visitors from all over the world.

Following the road-signs to the Childhood Cottage of Carl Nielsen, ten miles south of Odense, a pilgrim needs a well-informed local guide to point out a small, insignificant stone at the edge of a field. Nothing of note can be seen from this point, and the peace and calm is broken only occasionally by a passing car or tractor. The Nielsen devotee may check the small plain stone on which is inscribed 'Here stood the childhood cottage of Carl Nielsen.' The engraved stone is verified by Nielsen's own book, *Min fynske barndom* ('My Childhood on Fyn'), which states that here, at Sortelung in the parish district of Nørre-Lyndelse, there once stood a dilapidated farm-labourer's cottage. It was in the middle of a field, well off the road, and could be reached only by two footpaths; it housed two families. 'It was a mere hovel,' Nielsen wrote,

> … *but our half had two windows with rather larger panes. My mother was quite proud of this, and she always had pots of pretty flowers on the window-sills. I have no idea how we found space. Our cottage consisted of two rooms and a kitchen, and, as there were always eight of us children at home, I cannot understand, either, how we all contrived to eat at the same table, even leaving out the smallest. But we got on splendidly; we were always fit, healthy and happy, and there was a tidiness about our home that I know everybody in the neighbourhood admired.*

Outside the cottage, there was born under the night sky of 9 June 1865 the seventh child of Maren Kirsten, former house-maid, and Niels Jørgensen, called Niels Maler (the painter). Niels, who accepted work wherever he could find it, was never to stay long at home, and eight years after his marriage in 1855 he was conscripted. He survived as a veteran of the Danish–Prussian war of 1864, returning to his family on foot: the southern territories of Jylland (Jutland) had been lost, and a period of national gloom and shortages ensued.

Fyn, which had always been a backwater, was now a remote part of a country demoralized and aiming to consolidate itself after its defeat – but life in the region went on much as before. On 13 August 1865 Niels's son was baptized Carl August at the church at Nørre-Lyndelse. By a custom which was archaic even at the time he was given a surname, Nielsen, that was derived from his father's forename. Many accounts, which have glibly tried to explain Nielsen's music as a product of a rural childhood, inaccurately describe him as the off-spring of 'peasants'. His mother – Maren Kirsten Jørgensen, née

Nielsen's parents Niels Jørgensen, *right*, and Maren Kirsten Jørgensen (née Johansen), *above*

Johansen (1833–97) – was in fact the daughter of a wealthy family of sea captains from Seden, near Odense. She was working as a servant-girl when she met Niels and out of wedlock bore him a daughter, Jørgine Karoline, on 23 October 1854. Maren was much admired as a conscientious, warm-hearted and resourceful young woman. Unlike Niels, who avoided religious beliefs, she held strong Christian convictions fused with many superstitious principles from which (Nielsen conceded later) her children would probably never free themselves entirely. She married Niels on 29 November 1855 and subsequently bore him a further eleven children.

Niels Jørgensen (1835–1915) was free-thinking, energetic, unsettled, itinerant and of keen intelligence but he came from a lower walk of life than his wife. After his marriage he supplemented his labourer's income by playing cornet and violin at social functions. After Niels took a little alcohol, the music of the band was enhanced by his hilarious mimicry and storytelling with which rival bands could not compete. Niels's musical friends included the clarinet player 'Blind Anders' and the violinist Christian Larsen from Bellinge. Both men made an impact on the young Carl Nielsen: Anders was to be immortalized in the popular oratorio, *Fynsk foraar* ('Springtime on Fyn'), and Larsen was admired by the composer-to-be for his exceptional musical talent, which he had to sacrifice in order to run a family farm. In various groupings local players performed with Niels at the best local weddings and feasts; eventually dates of functions came to be changed to accommodate Niels's diary. He would join in the merriment of the functions at which he played late into the night, and under the effect of schnapps and ale his inhibitions completely vanished. One of Niels's compositions, *The Højby Riflemen's March*, written at the request of the politician Klaus Berntsen, has survived in an arrangement by his son.

In *Min fynske barndom* Carl Nielsen portrays his childhood as idyllic and in general he smooths over details of his parents' struggle for survival. But he admitted:

*... at times we would experience the greatest want. It was often serious. Once when my father was away from my home for a week, playing at weddings and christenings at Nyborg, Mother had no money left, so we had neither butter, dripping, nor meat to put on our bread, still less hot*

*food. She had bought some horse fat from a butcher, rendered it down and poured it into a big, reddish-brown earthenware jug to set. I can still see the yellowish surface of the dripping. Mother had cut some slices of bread and was standing with the bread-knife in her hand, about to spread the dripping. Then she could no longer restrain herself: I saw a big tear drop on to the rim of the jug and splash out like a star. Mother, however, quickly recovered herself, and said with a sort of smile, 'Well dears, I've nothing better to give you!' But when we had got the food and had sprinkled plenty of salt on it it was not so bad; but then I dare say we were pretty hungry.*

The Danish researcher Jørgen Larsen recently discovered records in Odense dating from 1862–74 which revealed that Niels's family was frequently obliged to apply for Poor Relief. The family depended on this although Nielsen's mother accepted it reluctantly, and only when her pride could be preserved. The local farmers, respectful of her pride, deliberately left fields with ears of corn (Carl helped his mother glean fields in the 1870s), and neighbours gave sausages directly to her children.

The parents made the most of things, however, an attitude which extended to the nourishment of their children's minds. As a small child, Carl noted the sounds of insects, animals, humans and machines with keen interest. The first music he heard was his mother singing. 'She had a voice that, while not strong, was clear and firm ... When she sang to herself there was a wistful note in her voice, as if she longed for something right over the farthest trees.' There can be no doubt that Nielsen's own compositional path was shaped by these experiences, not merely in a mimicking of nature, but also in the expression of 'many life-giving impressions that can refresh the mind and make all life pleasant'.

Carl Nielsen describes his brother Sophus, who was three years his elder, as

*... like all my brothers and sisters, very musical. He played the violin, but never got very far with it owing to the fact that his little finger had been crushed and because throughout his adolescence he was in farm service and looked after cows ... He loved animals, and the cows he tended ran after him like faithful dogs. Once when I visited him at his place in*

Carl Nielsen (left) with
three of his brothers, Peter,
Sophus and Anders

*the country, near Høby, I saw how his cows loved him. He sat on a gate
and blew some notes on a whistle he had cut for me. He did not say, 'This
is for you,' but he handed it to me and looked at me with his blue eyes.*

And Sophus 'would spend days walking about copses and woods,
watching birds and listening to their song. But occasionally what we
would hear would not be birdsong. He would occasionally break into
free musical fancy and make tunes of his own with many runs and
trills, and I doubt whether any music I have heard since has given me
so much sweetness, refinement and diversion.'

When Nielsen was aged five or six, the local farm-owner, Squire
Langkilde of the Bramstrup Estate, stopped by the cottage in his field
to chat to Nielsen's mother. Their conversation was halted by some
strange sounds. 'I was behind a stack of wood, playing tunes on
them,' Nielsen explained fifty-six years later. 'My brother and I had
made the discovery that the pieces had different notes. I had marked

the ends with chalk and, by hitting them with a hammer, could play various little tunes ... Mr Langkilde said, "You are a very clever boy!" and took my nose between his finger and thumb. But my mother having taught me to blow at this signal, I dutifully did so. With what result I cannot say, but the old gentleman laughed heartily ...'

Around this time Carl was confined to bed with measles. His mother handed him a three-quarter size violin which hung on the wall and suggested that he might try to follow some tunes she would sing. Each day when her housework was finished, she sat on Carl's bed, sang, and he would play. Maren was a hard taskmistress – whenever Carl did not play in tune she would tell him, 'No, now listen properly.' On his recovery he remembered that his mother had once invited him to take a close look at the kitchen table. When he did so he noticed that the grain of the wood was finer and closer than any other timber, 'so hard that you could make no impression in it with your fingernail'. Then his mother lifted the lid and removed dishes and utensils, revealing rows of long wires which the boy associated with the telegraph wires which ran through Høby station. When he plucked them with his fingers he was thrilled by the sounds that were produced, but his mother had little time for such play, so she replaced the dishes, and the kitchen 'table' – a broken-down harpsichord – was closed.

The first time Nielsen saw a real piano was an occasion he recalled vividly. His mother had a half-brother, Hans, who was well-known as the blind organist of Dalum Church near Odense. One day mother and son set out very early for the city, a walk of approximately seven miles. While she did some shopping in the town Carl waited for her near the harbour, then they both went to visit Uncle Hans. After Hans had accepted half a sausage and some eggs, the great moment arrived. He crossed the floor, opened the piano and invited the boy to try to play it.

'It was an ordinary upright, mahogany piano,' Nielsen recalled,

*... but it would be useless for me to attempt to describe the experience it was for me to touch the keys and gradually pick out tunes with one or two fingers. I would rather try to explain what I now think must be the reason for the unforgettable delight I felt at exploring the long row of keys that lay before me. After all, I had heard music before, heard Father play*

*the violin and cornet, heard Mother sing; and, when in bed with the
measles, I had tried on the little violin myself. But this was something
quite different. Here the notes lay in a long shining row before my eyes.
Not only could I hear them; I could see them. And I made one great
discovery after another. First of all, that the deep notes went to the left
and the high ones the other way. But I was at a loss to know what the
black pieces were for, and it was not until I had trouble with a tune
which in the middle had an F sharp instead of F natural that I made a
fresh discovery: that every bit had a meaning and that the black keys had
a meaning too … I cannot remember whether I found chords or triads,
but with one finger of each hand I played a long succession of sweet thirds,
and as my two fingers thus kept company I thought, remembering a snatch
of an old song, 'Two thrushes sat on a beech-tree branch.'*

While attending the local school, aged eight or nine, Carl attracted
the attention of the farm manager of the Langkilde Estate, who gave
him his first job. He became a goose-herd, a job with greater
responsibilities and trials than might be supposed. One day, he
recalled, he heard a cry in the sky, and looking up, he saw a flock of
wild geese or swans. His own herd of geese screeched, scattered and
flew over a tall hedge leaving the boy behind in tears of rage. But after
discovering an opening in the hedge, he finally caught up with them a
long way off. They were still agitated, cackling, and refused to be
rounded up. Eventually the animals were persuaded to return, but
they had to be squeezed back through the hole he had enlarged in the
hedge of thorns. They began to pass through the improvised passage
but in this way became stubbornly separated from the gander and
some of the oldest geese. Again, Carl wept. He found that he could
cut thorns away near a gate and so pushed one of them through; it
rewarded him by fouling his clothes. This youthful hardship,
chronicled fifty years later in *Min fynske barndom* was softened by a
new perspective on life's vicissitudes: 'This solitude, these tribulations
and tears, hold for me some of the poetry of heaven and earth.'

Following Denmark's defeat in 1864 and its cession of land to
Prussia, a programme of land drainage and modern agriculture was
organized by a new Danish government. The material conditions of
Carl Nielsen's country and family improved steadily. From about the
age of nine Carl took lessons on the violin from both his father and

Emil Petersen, the schoolmaster at Nørre-Lyndelse. Even before then, however, Nielsen had started to invent his own tunes. 'It was a great trouble to find out how to write them down. Before I learned notation I employed various symbols and words in order to fix my tunes – for instance, one long A, two short Ds, etc.' In his writings Nielsen (who in later years taught and actively encouraged young musicians) discussed the development of talent, stating that, if neglected, it would not only waste away but lead to dissatisfaction in later life.

Nielsen attributed most of his own musical talent and encouragement to his mother, but he also gave praise to his father as follows: '[He] had a rare sense of rhythm and played with the measured beat of a piston in a steam engine; for this reason he was known over central Fyn as the best dance-player ... If at such a feast the music was played by four or five musicians, my father would take the cornet, the instrument he really played best, having a brilliant *embouchure* and great stamina.' Niels's *The Højby Riflemen's March* was not the only composition in Carl Nielsen's ancestry: Niels's uncle, Jørgen Fællig, had also written several pieces. Of these, Carl Nielsen wrote, 'Two of his melodies are quite original in rhythm and composition. They have a sprightliness and grace reminiscent of Schubert ... Father used to say he could write down tunes he had never heard before after a single hearing.' As new dance-music from Copenhagen or Germany was expensive to purchase, Nielsen's great-uncle was both admired and reviled for impressively turning this aural ability to advantage. He would hide himself with sheets of ruled paper outside halls where rival dance bands were playing, and a few days later his own troupe could be heard playing the same tunes – usually in a far livelier style – much to the annoyance of the other bands.

A musical society called Braga (the Nordic god of the bards) was formed around 1873 by amateur musicians and teachers widely scattered across the district. Their objective was to learn about good music. The orchestra consisted of four violins, a viola, a cello, a double bass, a clarinet, a flute, two cornets, a trombone and a triangle or small drum – a good ensemble for light waltzes and polkas although the players occasionally tackled overtures and symphonic movements by Mozart and Haydn. Nielsen was allowed to attend the rehearsals and on one occasion played the triangle in H. C. Lumbye's *Dagmar Polka.*

Nielsen's earliest surviving composition originated at a feast in about 1874. He had to deputize for his father who was late in arriving, and so he played his own piece. No one had heard such music before. It was a polka, liberally syncopated. Niels entered the hall while it was being played, took out his violin, and began to support his son, but his face betrayed his true feelings. When the piece came to an end, his verdict was: 'You'd better stop this funny business, they can't dance to it.'

Around 1876 the estate demolished the dilapidated labourers' cottage in the middle of the field. Niels's family then moved into another cottage located on the far side of a local brick-field about twenty-five yards from some deep clay pits. Carl was one day playing with his youngest sister, Anna Dusina, aged two or three, when the little girl fell into one of the clay pits. He ran for his mother who arrived at the edge just in time to see Anna Dusina rise to the surface of the water, too far out to be reached. Maren ran round to the other side of the pit where the bank was lower but although the child surfaced again, then for a third time, she was still out of reach. Maren's fingers clutched at the ground in anguish. She closed in on a small branch with which she was able to draw in her daughter. Nielsen conceded, on reflection, that the existence of the branch was fortuitous, there being no shrubs nor trees in the vicinity, but when his mother spoke of the incident, she thanked the Lord for placing it there. Carl Nielsen belonged to a new generation with rational views on fate.

The new home was close to the manufacturing of clay bricks in a quarry where Carl obtained his next job. He then became a cow-herd for a farmer named Kresten Henriksen. He also helped his father mix the oils and pigments on stones to make paint, but had little aptitude and no liking for this. Playing with his father's musicians at weddings was a different matter. On one occasion Carl and his brother Sophus, aged thirteen and seventeen respectively, had played at a feast all night. Having successfully deputized for their father they began to walk home. Towards daybreak they became trapped in a blizzard and in exhaustion they fell asleep. Carl dreamed of a snake creeping down his neck, awoke to find snow melting inside his clothes and revived his brother. But for this dream, neither brother might have survived.

'They can't dance to it': Carl's father's comment on his son's first surviving composition, a polka for the violin

In Spring 1877 Carl was walking to Allested with his mother in a heat haze along the road from Nørre-Lyndelse to Nørre-Søby. She stopped and pointed out a cottage.

*It was a handsome, brick-built, thatched cottage with seven windows and a long, narrow garden intersected by the road ... My mother confided in me that she would like to own this house. I must have said something about it being quite beyond our means, for I remember word for word what she said. 'When we wish for something with all our hearts, we must keep on thinking of it, not talk about it, and we shall get it in the end' ... A year later we actually moved into this palace of sun and light and gladness.*

Land records show that Niels placed his deposit to purchase on 23 March 1878. But he and Maren could only eke out a living, forcing them three years later to sell up and emigrate to Chicago where two of their children, Anders Jacob and Julie Christine, had already established themselves. Niels and Maren spent their last years in Denmark, however, as they had been unable to adapt to the New World. But their son Carl would not even live for fifteen months in the cottage now preserved to immortalize his childhood. He was taking classes to prepare for his confirmation, after which he was to leave home to enter farm service or begin an apprenticeship. Although Nielsen states that he paid scant attention at these classes and learned very little about religion, one Pastor Briand succeeded (despite his

*Following page*, the cottage into which the Nielsen family moved in 1878 – 'a palace of sun and light and gladness'. Now preserved to commemorate Nielsen's childhood, it was the composer's home for less than fifteen months.

pupil's apathy) in having the boy confirmed at Easter 1879 in Heden Church, a chapel-of-ease to Nørre-Søby.

Carl immediately followed his brother Albert in becoming a grocer's assistant at Ellinge, near Nyborg, a job which failed to kindle his enthusiasm. He obtained a copy of Eibe's *100 Lessons in English* and resolved to escape to America. In the event, however, his employment came to an abrupt end after only three months. Three men, one with gold braid round his cap, entered the shop and summoned the grocer, who was dying of consumption, from his sick bed. Coughing badly, the grocer went through to the front shop where a bankruptcy notice was served on him. Carl then returned home to the cottage, but only for a brief period, because his father pointed out a vacancy for a regimental bugler in the 16th Battalion at Odense. The entrance examination was to be held in July or August 1879, which, he believed, would give a boy of his son's talent enough time to practise. To the delight of his proud parents, their fourteen-year-old was judged the best applicant, even though the two other boys competing were aged sixteen and eighteen. The great fear, however, was over Carl's health, as he had suffered from a persistent cough for about a year. Would the youngster fail the medical test? When the day of the test came, mother and son waited with great trepidation for the surgery door to open. A jovial doctor emerged and took hold of the boy. He recommended that the boy's lungs be examined if he was to be a hornblower. The lungs were pronounced perfectly satisfactory, but the mother was taken aside and asked if she did not seriously think that such a small fellow would pine for her.

Carl's doting mother was nervous on other grounds. Although one of her boys had emigrated as far as Australia, none of them had ever entered the world of soldiering. She warned Carl at length against all sorts of eventualities, including fallen women and the consequences of 'French disease' (which she compared to the smell of the rotten potatoes they occasionally dug up). Nielsen was also strongly advised to avoid a scoundrel notorious in the area, a bandsman called Jens Søby. If he was mindful of all of these things, he could join the regiment with his parents' blessing.

2

Nielsen the junior corporal,
c. 1880, with (from left to
right) his sister Sophie and
brothers Albert and Sophus

*Every musician is entitled to use tones as he
thinks fit. Old rules may be accepted or rejected
at will. Schoolmasters no longer take their
scholars by the ear; whipping and thrashing
have been abolished, abuse and scolding
silenced. But let no man assume that he can
relax his efforts on that account.*

Carl Nielsen, *Living Music*, 1925

## Bandsman and Musical Student 1879–89

In the summer of 1879 a new recruit, who was small in stature even
for the age of fourteen, was measured up for his uniform by the
regimental tailor. The boy was ordered to report to his immediate
superior, Chief Bugler Schreiber, at the band's depot in Odense.
Motivated by his unsophisticated country background he aimed to
equal or even exceed the standards of the somewhat supercilious
bigger boys. Lessons on the signal horn went well but he was handed
an E flat trombone which he did not master so readily. Any difficulties
he encountered were met by hard raps on the knuckles and a long
lecture on his duty to his country and to his parents.

   After the prescribed period of training in military music and drill,
two battalion bands were combined to form a regimental band and
Nielsen was ordered to attend a full rehearsal with his alto trombone.
He remembered the day vividly: 'The orchestra came in with a
*fortissimo*. I nearly sank to my knees at the dreadful din. It was like
being thrown into a raging sea inhabited by all sorts of monsters
that were dashing the spray over one another, crying and screaming,
pushing and buffeting and pulling one another's tails in one
mighty uproar.'

   Every few days it was Nielsen's turn to sound the reveille. On one
occasion Bugler 5 of Company 3 of the 16th Battalion reported six
minutes late for duty, for which he duly received a reprimand. Apart
from this lapse his progress was exemplary. Only one of his colleagues
could match his ability to sound the signals properly, and it was a real
boost to Nielsen's self-confidence that he was able to hold the top
notes for almost one minute, or so he claimed. Stationed at Odense,
Nielsen was permitted to earn pocket money, off-duty, as one of his
father's musicians at celebrations. He continued with his violin
lessons and played string quartets by Haydn, Mozart, Pleyel and
Georges Onslow.

   In 1880 new regulations paved the way for his early promotion to
the rank of lance-corporal. This embarrassed the older boys, who

stiffly had to salute their 'senior' who now sported a white stripe and a gleaming button on the sleeve of his coat. The promotion increased Carl's earnings and enabled him to move to private lodgings. His pay during the first year was a very lowly 2 DKr and 95 øre per week plus an 8lb loaf of rye bread every five days. Subsistence was managed by trading some of this bread with his landlady for other foodstuffs, and

Nielsen aged sixteen, with signal horn and trombone, after his promotion to junior corporal

receiving some sausage, eggs and salt-meat from his mother's visits. He made a special arrangement with an inn-keeper who calculated that 20 øre for a hot meal was a fair price to charge a youngster who came from his own home town. Nielsen was now able to fulfil a long-held ambition. With the consent of his landlady, he purchased a piano for 50 DKr, which he had seen in a watchmaker's shop in Overgade. It was a little flat piano, as he described it, 'very modest-looking, but all the notes were there and it played in tune.' The vendor was prepared to accept Nielsen's savings of 20 DKr as a deposit and the balance was then paid by instalments of 1 DKr per week. Nielsen even had enough money to buy some cheap piano tutors and second-hand music, including a sonata in C major by Mozart and Part I of Johann Sebastian Bach's *The Well-Tempered Clavier*.

At this time Nielsen became acquainted with an elderly gentleman who was the pianist in a basement tavern in Vestergade. Nielsen was subsequently to say that it was from this man – known as Outzen – that he acquired his first strong impressions of good music. The son of a senior customs official from Schleswig-Holstein, Outzen was well-versed in music and literature but found himself in straitened circumstances thanks to a bad marriage and the effects of drink. In the tavern after hours, the two played the easiest of Mozart's and Beethoven's sonatas for violin and piano as Nielsen's technique at this stage was not very advanced. When he admitted to difficulties with *The Well-Tempered Clavier*, Outzen told him that Bach was deep and strange and that his music was best left until Nielsen was much older. Naturally, the young Carl set out to study this music the next day, but for a long time, as Outzen had predicted, it meant nothing to him. 'In Red Indian stories I had read how the savages lit a fire by rubbing two sticks together till they began to smoulder. The same thing happened to me,' Nielsen recalled. 'When I had played the little E flat minor Prelude No. 8 some fifty times I suddenly caught fire. The door was open now, and I could begin exploring an entirely new and strange world. But I left Bach again when Outzen began to teach me the piano, and was in my mid twenties before I again tackled *The Well-Tempered Clavier*.'

By 1881, when Nielsen was sixteen, he was taking violin lessons from Carl Larsen, the Director of the Odense Music Society, and had formed a string quartet. A cluster of compositions date from this period in the early 1880s – some pieces for horn, trumpet, alto and tenor trombones, a Sonata for Violin and Piano, and a String Quartet. In later years its composer would consider the quartet to be surprisingly well-formed, 'the scherzo having a correctly executed canon,' but he acknowledged that it was lacking in originality. The music for brass instruments was encouraged by none other than Jens Søby, the degenerate bandsman from whom Carl's mother had warned her son to keep his distance at all costs. At the concert combining the two bands, Carl had been paired with 'the bad influence' who, as luck had it, also played the E flat trombone. Once or twice their eyes met but Nielsen looked away, planning in detail how he would avoid any discussions, invitations, or temptations. Although this man was destined for downfall, he ironically became Nielsen's protector against the bullies and their bad language. They became close friends, which was especially surprising given an age difference they perceived as vast – all of six years. With remarkable maturity for his age, the young Nielsen soon formed his own opinion of Søby:

*He fascinated me – like a boiling pot, all bubbling with thick, unclean scum, yet coming into its own by reason of the fire, steam, warmth and vitality therein. He was always either wholly alert and interested, or dull and listless, like grey ashes on the site of a fire. He once spoke to me about himself, saying he was condemned to lead a dissolute life … I was not to bother my head about that … But I might be able to get somewhere in my art, if I guarded myself against bad influences and worked hard at it.*

Nielsen started to develop his interest in literature by taking a weekly journal called *Revuen*. He was stirred by translations of English novels, especially Bulwer-Lytton's *Harold, the Last of the Saxon Kings*; and among Danish writers, he favoured the novelist and lyrical poet Steen Steensen Blicher. But, dissatisfied with his military career and disappointed by the lack of opportunity in Odense to make musical progress, he yielded for a short time to the adolescent temptations and diversions of the wilder youths as he approached his seventeenth year somewhat aimlessly. His mother's warnings, confirmed even by Jens Søby, helped to save him from too much degenerate behaviour, but he was as yet no nearer knowing what to do with his life.

His thoughts began to turn towards Copenhagen following the
visit to Odense of a famous bandleader and composer of light music,
Olfert Jespersen, with his company of singers. Nielsen met Jespersen
in the tavern where Outzen played, and invited him back to his room
which was so small that their performance together of one of Nielsen's
compositions was awkward. But on the strength of this, Jespersen,
highly impressed by the force of the young man's musicality, told him
that with formal training he would certainly have a future in music.
Denmark's Conservatoire of Music, founded in 1866 in Copenhagen,
was known to Nielsen but studying there was quite beyond the means
of his parents. By this time, however, he was a handsome, well-
mannered young corporal, who was very accomplished in music, and
a regular guest in the homes of some of Odense's well-to-do. A few
of these wealthy people grouped together anonymously to offer him
financial assistance if he were to pass the entrance examination. The
local politician Klaus Berntsen made all the necessary arrangements,
and Nielsen was granted five days' leave to travel by sea to
Copenhagen in civilian clothes.

This rite of passage took place on a sunny day in May 1883. Time
on board ship was spent practising the double stops in *Souvenir de
Boulogne*, a piece for solo violin by the Belgian virtuoso and ped-
agogue, Hubert Léonard. Once in Copenhagen Nielsen checked into
a cramped hotel. The following morning, to his great excitement, he
found the road cordoned off for another visitor to the city, Alexander
III, Tsar of Russia. Nielsen walked to the home of the violin professor,
Valdemar Tofte, where the required audition was to take place.
A pupil of the great virtuoso Joseph Joachim, Tofte was charming
and immediately put the boy at his ease, telling him that he played
nicely and in tune, and that there was no reason why he should
not be admitted to the Conservatoire. But he had first to submit his
quartet to the Conservatoire's director, Professor Gade.

Nielsen set out on foot for the home of Niels W. Gade the next
day. It is almost an understatement to say that Gade (1817–90) was
Denmark's foremost musician and composer. As a young prodigy,
he had received a government stipend to study in Leipzig, where he
became a close friend of Felix Mendelssohn and conducted the
Gewandhaus Orchestra after the latter's death in 1847. War forced
Gade's hasty return to Copenhagen, where, through his own
compositions, Danish composers became influenced by the Leipzig

Klaus Berntsen, educator
and politician, sponsored
Nielsen's admission to the
Royal Danish Conservatoire.

school. In 1866 Gade jointly founded the Royal Danish Conservatoire
of Music with J. P. E. Hartmann and H. S. Paulli.

Arriving at Gade's home soon after lunchtime, Nielsen was ushered
in by a maid. The professor was very busy and, having read the
letter from Klaus Berntsen, said that Nielsen should go to see Tofte.
The boy was intimidated but succeeded in saying that he had
already done so and that he had now brought to Gade one of his
own compositions, a string quartet. Gade agreed to examine one
movement from it and Nielsen hastily retrieved the Andante from
his violin case. The professor turned the score towards the window,
showing neither approval nor contempt, but his lips pursed as if to
whistle silently or hum the tunes. Handing back the music when he
had finished, Gade said that the movement showed Nielsen's good
sense of form and that he could be admitted to the Conservatoire if
he passed the violin test. As Nielsen already knew that he had satisfied
Tofte with regard to his violin playing, he was elated by a new sense
of purpose.

Niels W. Gade (1817–90),
composer and founder-
director of the Royal Danish
Conservatoire

He returned to Odense to face two further obstacles: obtaining an early discharge from his regiment and persuading his parents that he should give up a secure position for an uncertain future. He chose to confront his mother and father separately with the momentous news. At first his mother seemed very concerned but, after much anguished discussion, she ended by whispering some words he could barely hear but would never forget: 'I think you can do it.'

Nielsen waited several weeks before approaching his father. They were to play at a fête and Nielsen had travelled by train to Pederstrup Station, only to find that the others had already gone ahead. He took a short-cut, carrying his violin and trombone across a rye field. In these beautiful surroundings he hesitated for a moment, and allowed all his misgivings about leaving the island, opposing his father and missing his mother, to come to the surface. At the fête the politician Klaus Berntsen rose to make a speech, and as he invariably spoke for at least half an hour, Nielsen took the opportunity to take his father aside. It was not long before the boy felt guilty for having instigated matters but he resisted his father's arguments, which were many and strong. When Carl confirmed that he had not yet applied for military discharge, Niels seemed relieved, only to hear the retort from Carl that there was no real alternative in the end. Father gave son an intense look, and no more words were exchanged.

In December 1883 Nielsen passed the Conservatoire's formal examination with an exemption from paying fees. He enrolled, and was due to begin his music studies on 1 January 1884. He spent Christmas at the new cottage, the symbol of his family's and his country's improved economic circumstances. As each day passed, he realized increasingly that his rural childhood had come to an end.

Many years later, when his life in Copenhagen became oppressive, he described the island to which he so often longed to return:

The Royal Danish Conservatoire of Music, founded in 1866 – eighteen years before Nielsen enrolled there

*Some laugh at the dialect of Fyn, but they have no ear for its matchless song ... Everything in Fyn is different from the rest of the world, and whoever takes the trouble to listen will know. The bees hum in a way of their own with a special accent, and when the horse whinnies and the red*

*cows low, why, anybody can hear that it is quite different from anywhere else. It is a lilting Fyn that the throstle flutes, and the laughter of the blackbird as it slips under the lilac bushes is an imitation of the starling's whims, themselves an echo of the enchanting chuckle of the girls of Fyn when they jest and laugh in the gardens behind the clipped hedges. The bells ring and the cocks crow in the dialect of Fyn, and a joyous symphony issues from all the birds' nests every time the mother bird feeds her young.*

By the time Nielsen arrived in Copenhagen as a student in 1884, the effects of the spirit of recovery following the 1864 defeat were tangible. But it is appropriate first to recall the events which led up to 1864. Governmental reorganization had started even earlier with the events of 1848. Under the influence of the French and German revolutions in February and March, absolute monarchy ended in Denmark on the death of Christian VIII in January 1849. The Danish Constitution of June preserved the institution of monarchy, but guaranteed freedom of the press, worship, meetings and free association. A new parliament with two chambers of equal legislative power was established, elected by all Danish men over thirty: the *Landsting* (upper house), which required its members to be property owners, and the *Folketing* (lower house). The courts, which had always been an efficient dispenser of justice, retained their independence.

After ceding Norway, Denmark's patriotic feelings focused on Schleswig-Holstein and the long-standing problem of the sovereignty of those territories. Although government had always been exercised from Denmark, both Schleswig and Holstein were duchies. Whereas Holstein was a member of the German Confederation, Schleswig was culturally and linguistically divided. In 1848 the Danish Liberal government decided to resist the movement within Schleswig to free itself from Danish rule and affiliate with Holstein and German confederacy. Both sides resorted to arms, and a war was fought over three summers. As the rebels received military aid from Prussia, Denmark could not hope to win and the first of the two wars ended when she signed treaties ambiguously agreeing to treat Schleswig as equal to Holstein, with the other major European powers as guarantors.

In 1863 Denmark gambled that Prussia was preoccupied with the Polish uprising against Russia and, confident of support from the

Copenhagen in 1864, during the Second Danish-Prussian War

Swedes, passed an Act of Constitution on 13 November separating Holstein and declaring sovereignty to vest equally with the kingdom of Denmark and the duchy of Schleswig. The risks of provocation were well-known, but tension turned to panic when Frederik VII died without issue, and before signing the Act. By the treaty of 1852 which was being flouted by this attempt to annex territory, Christian IX ascended the throne. It was in this climate that a new politician, Otto von Bismarck, decided to test his strength and mobilize his troops. By the end of February 1864 the whole of Jylland was occupied and the outcome was determined in favour of Germany by the Treaty of Vienna. The immediate consequence of this 'defeat' was the loss of land, the dismissal of the government and economic shortages.

After twenty years the gloom lifted like a mist to reveal the benefits of modernization. Denmark had seen herself reduced to Europe's smallest nation, facing the possibility of being carved up between Sweden and Germany in the event of further decline. National improvement began with the conversion of the barren moors of Jylland into forests and farms. To challenge the cheap corn and cattle flooding the world markets from the vast prairies of America, the country's agricultural efforts were organized into high quality dairy produce. Successful co-operatives ensured uniform quality and

Canons being pulled uphill
during the Second
Danish – Prussian War,
depicted in a painting of
1864 by N. Simonsen

effective marketing; the farmers participated in the operation and shared in the profits of the wholesale enterprise. Similar improvements followed in shipping and ship-building. Motorized fishing cutters replaced quaint old open boats. True to the post-war motto of 'what has been outwardly lost must be inwardly won' was the rise of the celebrated Folk High Schools, a result of the enlightened educational views of Bishop Grundtvig (1783–1872).

The city of Copenhagen was well-placed to benefit from her modernization. She flourished culturally and commercially as the crossroads between a Baltic and Slavonic eastern Europe, and an Austro–Hungarian central Europe. To the south were the Mediterranean countries and to the north Britain and the rest of Scandinavia. Influences from all of these lands may be seen in Copenhagen's art and architecture, a variety which sharpened the quest for indigenous styles.

Danish music was dominated by the currents from Germany, France and Italy until the beginning of the nineteenth century, when an independent Scandinavian style was fashioned principally by Gade as well as by J. P. E. Hartmann (1805–1900), and C. E. F. Weyse (1774–1842). When Carl Nielsen enrolled at the Royal Danish Conservatoire of Music, two Norwegians had also begun to influence the new Danish music further away from the central- or southern-European styles and sonorities. They were Edvard Grieg (1843–1907) and Johan Svendsen (1840–1911). The latter had moved to Copenhagen and raised its Royal (Chapel) Orchestra to a position of pre-eminence, introducing to its repertoire many European symphonic and operatic works. Nielsen arrived in Copenhagen only ten years after the opening of its palatial new Theatre Royal on the Kongens Nytorv (King's New Square). The Conservatoire of Music had been founded in 1866. Svendsen, like Gade, had trained in Leipzig and had returned to Denmark in 1870, settling there until his retirement as chief conductor at the Theatre Royal in 1908. The Leipzig influence on Danish composers was therefore doubly strong.

So when Nielsen arrived from somewhere near Odense, Gade was securely at the helm of a 'Scandinavian–Romantic' school but it was threatened on two counts. Firstly, the Leipzig connection was dominated by Mendelssohn and rooted in Schumann and thus founded on influences from a country for which Danes had little

The composers Johan Svendsen, *above*, and Edvard Grieg, *right*, were important influences on Danish music during Nielsen's education at the Conservatoire.

affection. Secondly, the music of Gade and Hartmann was criticized by some of their students as archaic, other-worldly, lacking in realism, and even weak or effeminate. The reformers had, however, been unable to define an independent direction which modern Scandinavian operas and symphonies should take. The Danish song tradition had also reached a turning point. It had its roots in Weyse and J. A. P. Schulz (1747–1800), and had reached a plateau with Gade, Hartmann and two notable Danish song-writers, Peter Heise (1830–79) and Peter Erasmus Lange-Müller (1850–1926).

The reformers, and the first circle of supporters of Nielsen's ideas, were drawn principally from his peers, many of whom became notable musical personalities: Victor Bendix, Rudolph Bergh, Hilda Sehested and Hugo Seligman. They were all fellow pupils of a gifted and influential teacher of music, their mentor Orla Rosenhoff (1845–1905), who taught music theory at the Danish Conservatoire from 1881 to 1892. He was the only teacher Nielsen greatly respected, and the only one to whom he felt that he owed anything. After Nielsen graduated

he continued to have private tuition from Rosenhoff, whose ear for
new music and whose concern for his pupils' progress made him a
good friend and guide to Nielsen until his death. It was to Orla
Rosenhoff that Nielsen dedicated two of his most important
early compositions.

Hilda Sehested, a pianist who studied under Rosenhoff, was later
to write an article on the occasion of Nielsen's sixtieth birthday
describing the restlessness and sense of expectation felt by her
contemporaries at that time. She described how Nielsen absorbed
from his three years at the Conservatoire only what was close to his
interests and what might be of direct use to his own artistic growth.
In his later years Nielsen would admit to Henrik Knudsen, the
pianist who became one of his closest friends and helpers, that his
Conservatoire years were not industrious and that he only took
from his lessons what he thought he might need.

He had started at the Conservatoire by plunging into hard work,
but later disclosed the true reason for this industry to a friend.

Orla Rosenhoff, Nielsen's
friend and mentor
at the Conservatoire

Shortly before he left Odense Nielsen had fallen madly in love with a young girl. Separated from her by such a distance, however, Carl had needed to study hard in order to forget her. Not long afterwards he heard that her parents, whom he disparaged as uneducated, had forced her to marry a rich leather merchant. This whole experience shattered his ideas of love for a long time, and he admitted of having had a dream, however foolish it might appear, of becoming a famous musician, returning to Odense and snatching the girl away from the merchant.

Considering Nielsen's struggle to reach the Conservatoire, his selective approach to its teaching is perhaps surprising. But he was disappointed in the Danish musical establishment. Dating from his days as a student, Copenhagen's musical narrowness oppressed him. It also became apparent that he would not be totally fulfilled as a violinist: a great deal of the repertoire simply did not interest him. In later years Nielsen would also confide to Henrik Knudsen that he was judged by his contemporaries to play the violin with an accurate but not beautiful tone. He was to begin composing music in earnest immediately after his graduation, but his formal courses while at the Conservatoire did not include composition. Presumably this had seemed too ambitious for a modest country boy. Almost certainly he would have found it stifling.

Nielsen's major subject was violin, under Tofte. He studied theory under J. P. E. Hartmann and Rosenhoff, history under Gade and piano under the organist J. Gottfred Mathison-Hansen. But it was under Rosenhoff's inspiration that Nielsen and other students became aware of limitations in the nineteenth-century Scandinavian musical style. Nielsen read widely beyond his curriculum, toured the art galleries and could often be seen playing in amateur string quartets. He became deeply absorbed in Copenhagen life and many of his important friendships date from this time.

Nielsen did not distinguish himself at the Conservatoire and he graduated in 1886 with a second-class degree. This qualified him to deputize in local orchestras and take some elementary private pupils. A few small-scale compositions emerged in the three years after his graduation. By 1887 he had turned his ambitions from performing to composing music: a cluster of works have been attributed to this year which indicates that he had time on his hands, and his source of income during these years remains a mystery. Although he seems to have forgotten the event in later years, his début as a composer consisted of two movements written for a string quartet, Andante Tranquillo and Scherzo. The scores are undated but they were performed by the string orchestra of the Tivoli Hall on 17 September 1887.

Carl Nielsen aged eighteen, in 1883; his grave demeanour disguises his natural warmth and good humour.

The next year began promisingly for Nielsen with the performance
on 25 January of his String Quartet in F major (1887) at the Privat
Kammermusikforening (Private Chamber Music Society); and in the
autumn the composer of a *Little Suite for Strings* was listed in the
national newspaper, *Politiken*, as 'a Mr Carl Nielsen whom nobody
knows'. It was performed on 8 September 1888 by the Tivoli Orchestra
conducted by the Danish conductor Balduin Dahl, and on 14 October
in Odense City Hall conducted by the composer himself. It was much
appreciated and brought Nielsen some real hope of success as a
composer. 'I still remember my fright when Dahl took me by the
scruff of my neck,' Nielsen recalled in *Politiken* in 1927. Few opus
ones are so self-assured. Written in three movements, the concise
Prelude begins in serious mood in the musical dialect of Grieg and
Svendsen. The waltz-like Intermezzo combines restraint with
an effusive self-confidence. Most progressive in form was the Finale,
in which the Suite's opening theme re-emerges with remarkable
ingenuity, a technique which Nielsen was to develop further.

While the first audiences appreciated this novelty from an
unknown, professional musicians reacted with caution. The contemporary Danish violinist, Frederik Schnedler-Petersen, recorded
Nielsen's disappointment when Gade severely criticized the *Little
Suite*, having already disparaged his pupil's G minor String Quartet,
composed in 1887–8. 'Little Nielsen,' he said, 'your work is still
too muddled.' But in the G minor String Quartet, which was performed on 18 December 1889 by the Chamber Music Society,
Nielsen had glimpsed the horizons beyond the boundaries charted by
his predecessors – the musical syntax of Beethoven, the structural
architecture of Brahms and the tones of Svendsen.

In 1889 the *Little Suite for Strings* was published by the firm of
Wilhelm Hansen, the leading Danish music publishers, and dedicated
to Rosenhoff. Some of his colleagues were encouraging, but others
were envious of the publication of an early work. Nielsen's *Little Suite*
remains a popular piece in its own right, but for Nielsen not only was
it the work that first brought him to public attention as a composer,
but it marked the important step from chamber to orchestral music.
Between this and the remarkably bold First Symphony of 1892, the
only orchestral music written was an abandoned single movement

The Tivoli Hall in
Copenhagen was the
setting for Nielsen's
debut as a composer
in 1887.

headed 'Symphony', an Allegro in F major, dated 1888, and bearing a dedication to his fellow pupil Victor Bendix. (It is now called the *Symphonic Rhapsody* and is infrequently performed.)

While he was under postgraduate instruction from Rosenhoff, Nielsen wrote songs. Some were for mens' choirs and set to words by the up-and-coming Danish poet, Jens Peter Jacobsen. Six songs from 1887 (unpublished but preserved in the Carl Nielsen Archive) were similar to the unpretentious and uncluttered examples his teacher himself composed and prescribed as exercises for his pupils. Nielsen was to set his melodies almost exclusively to Danish texts, but the earliest songs were exceptionally set to foreign poems, translated by Caralis (C. Preetzmann), of Byron, Shelley and Robert Burns (he was particularly successful with his setting of Burns's *Beware o' Bonny Ann*, since Burns's lowland Scots tongue closely echoes the sound and rhythm of the Danish language).

In 1889 Nielsen helped to establish Symphonia, the precursor of the Danish Young Composers' Society, which aimed to provide a public forum for new and unknown Danish works. This period of relative unemployment came to an end when on 1 September 1889, aged twenty-four, Nielsen gained the prospect of full-time employment by winning a place to join the second violin section of Det Kongelige Kapel (the Royal Chapel, now the Royal Danish Orchestra). Johan Svendsen, since his appointment as conductor in 1883, had brought it to a position of pre-eminence in Scandinavia with a wide repertoire of symphonies and operas. To the young Carl Nielsen this was a great achievement. He must have felt that at last he had arrived.

*3*

Carl Nielsen in his twenties;
at this age the young
composer was already
producing music of
'uncommon fantasy,
invention and originality'.

*... when one reflects on the great artists of the
past one seems to be conscious of two main types.
One, grave and gloomy, his brows contracted
and hands clenched, strides heavily and deter-
minedly forward. The other comes swinging
along with light springy steps, free and easy with
a friendly smile, as if walking in the sun.*

Carl Nielsen, *Living Music*, 1925

## Formative Travels 1889–91

'A stay abroad would, at my present phase and age ... have a broaden-
ing and stimulating effect on me.' This is what Nielsen wrote in
December 1888 when applying for the C. A. Ancker travel scholarship,
and the following year, while still a musician-at-large, he was awarded
1,800 Danish kroner. The ensuing study trip through the major cities
of Germany, France and Italy was Nielsen's first journey abroad and
it provided all that he had eagerly anticipated in his application.
While he was making preparations for the journey he had been
informed of his place in the second violin section of the Royal
Orchestra (to commence 1 September 1889), but he was granted leave
of absence to pursue his study trip.

During his travels Nielsen heard a wide spectrum of music, and
through contacts in the musical community and letters of introduction from Gade he formed lasting friendships with some of
Europe's leading musicians. Most of them heard Nielsen's music for
the first time – either in semi-professional recitals or through
playing chamber music. His diary reveals that his days were carefully
planned and filled to the brim with visits to art galleries, concerts,
meetings and socializing, but he also managed to complete a string
quartet and begin important new compositions. The musical and
cultural experiences of the trip inspired him with many ideas that
emerged fully realized in the seminal works of his first creative decade.
But he was critical of other music-makers: 'It is as if all my pores are
open when I am on a journey. That doesn't apply to music: there
I am always sceptical and cold, and feel no enrichment because
I constantly feel that I can both conduct and compose better ...'

On 3 September 1890 Nielsen set out on the study tour, travelling
by rail from Copenhagen to Berlin where he was welcomed into
several musical circles. He had already decided to concentrate his
efforts on studying the works of Richard Wagner, and in Berlin found
himself in the midst of the great debate concerning the direction that
music should take. Should it develop along the classical formal lines of

Haydn, Mozart and Beethoven, a tradition championed by Brahms,
or should it respond to the challenge set by Wagner – a revolutionary
synthesis of music, poetry, painting and drama? By the latter half
of the nineteenth century Wagner's operas might better be described
as ambitious music-dramas on a huge scale. Brahms was the better
known of the two composers in Denmark, especially through his
chamber music, but in Germany there was wild speculation about
the whole classical tradition being transformed by Wagner's fusion of
the arts. Before arriving in Berlin Nielsen had heard only two of
Wagner's operas, *Tannhäuser* and *Lohengrin*, and knew none of his
later music-dramas. When Nielsen heard all of Wagner's massive *Ring
of the Nibelungen* on four consecutive evenings in Berlin he was
overwhelmed. '… Wagner. He is a master! Great God, what a giant in
our times. It is incomprehensible that there are people who do not like
his music. I was not really so enthusiastic about him when I arrived
here … but now I cannot find words strong enough to praise him. He
is an immense genius. Hats off!'

It was in Germany that Nielsen also listened to orchestral works by
Richard Strauss, probably for the first time. His music, next to the
Classicism of Brahms, expressed more exuberant feelings and
emotions and was written in the less strictly symphonic form of the
'tone poem'. Briefly introduced to Strauss, who was only one year his
senior, Nielsen was impressed by his contemporary conducting his
own work, *Death and Transfiguration*, with the Berlin Philharmonic
Orchestra. But in spite of his admiration Nielsen's music was not even
temporarily influenced by that of Strauss.

The Dane preferred Dresden to Berlin, in atmosphere, its musical
standards and its friendly people. There he visited the famous violinist
J. C. Lauterbach, regretting that he had postponed the meeting until
he had learned to speak a little German. Before he left Dresden he
heard *Lohengrin*. 'The scene where day breaks and life begins to stir is
one of the most wonderful things I have seen or heard,' he wrote
home to his teacher Rosenhoff on 24 November 'Then I heard
Goldmark's *The Queen of Sheba*. No! Mere effect music … Wagner
imitators are the worst of all and Goldmark is tarred with the same
brush.' Holding in high esteem the opera of Dresden, Nielsen
returned to Berlin and was there deeply impressed by Wagner's *Die
Meistersinger*: '… magnificent! The second act is for me the greatest

comic music that exists. I had not believed that Wagner possessed such an overwhelmingly comic gift. How great he is.' When Nielsen's ardent enthusiasm for Wagner was tempered in later years by strong criticisms, it was this opera he considered to be the master's greatest, and the 'most likely to survive the longest' because it was 'healthy'.

Nielsen of course plunged into the great Brahms–Wagner controversy of the musical age. After hearing the Joachim Quartet play one of Brahms's string quartets, he enraged a young and talented cellist by commenting that he had found its finale a little dull. The cellist demanded of Nielsen what he knew of Brahms, but Nielsen turned the tables on the cellist by forcing him to admit that he had only heard two of Wagner's works. The cellist reverted to his original tack – no one should criticize a finale like this one by Brahms unless he could write such a thing. Eventually Nielsen won the heated argument because his opponent admitted he had never heard any of Nielsen's own finales!

Nielsen also made an exhaustive study of the Berlin art galleries. He recorded his reactions to modern works and to the old masters whose impact compared to the reproductions he had seen exceeded his highest expectations. He told Rosenhoff of Berlin's slackness compared to Dresden. 'The orchestra often plays each in his own way, but that doesn't worry a fat, phlegmatic Kapellmeister named Sucher ... Bülow is, on the other hand, a master. Great God! How he can handle an orchestra! Among the important works I have heard under his baton are ... Brahms's C minor symphony (twice), B flat Piano Concerto (twice), Beethoven's Eighth, Mozart's D major, Wagner's *Faust Overture*, Saint-Saëns's Cello Concerto ...' The list was impressive.

It was in Berlin in 1890 that Nielsen wrote three pieces for piano, supplementing two which he had already written at home. His Five Piano Pieces thus comprised: 1. Folk Tune 2. Humoresque 3. Arabesque 4. Mignon and 5. Elf Dance. Nielsen was flattered when word of his piano compositions reached Henrik Hennings, a music publisher who was visiting Berlin. Nielsen was invited to dinner by Hennings and became light-headed with champagne, which he was not used to in Denmark. In spite of being flattered, however, he felt a loyalty towards Alfred Hansen, proprietor of the leading Danish music publishers. Although Hansen had not yet offered him a term or exclusive contract, Nielsen was grateful to the firm for having published the *Little Suite for Strings* and the Fantasy Pieces for Oboe and Piano, so he kept his head and pretended that the piano studies had already been promised to Mr Hansen. The rival publisher persisted: he had been informed by local musicians who had heard the pieces that the Arabesque (the third of the Five Pieces) was especially fine, and he asked Nielsen to name his price but on condition that the works be printed by Christmas. This reassuring flattery went to Nielsen's head more than the champagne, but he nevertheless decided to place his future with Mr Hansen. Hennings was right about the Arabesque, which was outstanding in its originality and its haunting, lingering melody. According to Nielsen, the piece caused 'quite a stir'. Nielsen's first published piano compositions were in the mould of the popular short Romantic piano pieces by Mendelssohn and Schumann with the added influence of Hartmann, Gade and Grieg. But according to Arne Skjold Rasmussen, the distinguished Danish pianist, in the Arabesque are found 'figures and ideas which were to be the basic principles of Nielsen's later piano style'. The illumination of an unusual tonal design through fluid rhythm and metre would be characteristic of many of Nielsen's future works.

In addition to two of the Five Piano Pieces, Nielsen had left home with an unfinished string quartet in F minor which had taken longer than usual to perfect. 'Finished,' he noted in his diary entry for 13 November after he had revised the slow movement several times, 'but will it be understood? Here, even Svendsen … is not understood, so what will become of me?' Ten days later Nielsen wrote to Rosenhoff: 'After the première at the Hochschule I will send you the whole Quartet. It's a wonderful feeling to have finished a big work, but it's strange that each time this has happened to me, I have a feeling of being on the point of a beginning. It doesn't tire me. On the contrary, it gives me strength!'

A month after its completion, the quartet was performed before an invited audience including the highly influential violin virtuoso and teacher, Joseph Joachim, at his Königliche Hochschule für Musik in Berlin. Nielsen played first violin and the other performers included two visiting Danish musicians, the violinist Fini Henriques and the viola player Frederik Schnedler-Petersen. An American, John Paul Morgan, played the cello. Despite five rehearsals, Nielsen was disappointed by the performance, which was given one week before Christmas. 'Joachim ... suggested that I revise the quartet; but indeed, I will not. Its time will come.' The maestro's opinion of Nielsen was that he had 'an uncommon fantasy, invention and originality', but that there were so many terribly radical passages that he would have to break away from this tendency. The following day, Joachim took the trouble to discuss the quartet with Nielsen in some detail. Except for

The violin virtuoso Joseph Joachim (1831–1907), in a sketch by J. Karbina. 'Write what you will, so long as you feel it,' was Joachim's advice to Nielsen.

one spot, 'where Joachim was right over a trifle', many points where he suggested the score might be rewritten were the elements which on the contrary most pleased Nielsen. The composer retorted to Joachim that the whole quartet would lose its character if his suggested changes were made. Nielsen reported all this to Rosenhoff, saying that he had expected some angry response from the older man as he would have received at home from Gade, but Joachim had replied in a kindly tone: 'Yes, dear Herr Nielsen, maybe I am a real old Philistine. Write what you will, so long as you feel it.'

Although the quartet still bore traces of Brahms and Svendsen, it represented a big step towards the discovery of Nielsen's own style and as such is a major advance on its predecessor, written only two years before. The radical nature of the work (commented on by Joachim) lay in the presentation of thematic material, which was more tightly structured and more concisely stated than before. The composer was certainly finding his own voice within one of the most rigorous musical genres.

Four days after the recital in Berlin, bad news arrived from Copenhagen: Gade had died on 21 December. Nielsen's shock and grief were recorded in his diary. By this time Gade's music was already out of fashion in Germany but as a personality he was much loved, and his demise turned the letter of introduction in Nielsen's hands into a key to all the musical doors in Germany. Nielsen continued his travels. Despite the acclaim for the F minor String Quartet, it did not receive its first public performance until 8 April 1892 at a concert given by the Royal Orchestra in Copenhagen; twenty days later it was given another performance at an all-Nielsen concert with two collections of songs, all settings of poems by J. P. Jacobsen. The Quartet was published that year by Alfred Hansen, with a dedication to Anton Svendsen, the violinist who had led the work in its première.

The String Quartet justified Nielsen's self-confidence and carried his name across Europe and America. Later, in 1894, when Nielsen visited Germany to conduct his First Symphony, he was delighted when the great Belgian violinist Eugène Ysaye demonstrated that it really was Nielsen's quartet that he had heard and was determined to purchase a copy. He only convinced the doubting Nielsen by whistling the main theme of its first movement.

Just before he had set off on the study-trip, Nielsen had fallen in love a second time, again with a young girl from Odense. After the recital with Joachim, when briefly confined by illness around Christmas 1890 in Berlin, Nielsen wrote to his close friend Emil B. Sachs, warning him to stand by for an imminent engagement announcement. Parting from her had made up his mind. But fate took another turn. At the end of February 1891, he arrived in Paris, a city which Nielsen was always to find emotionally and artistically inspiring, and met the students of the Scandinavian Society. The painter Augusta Dolman informed a Danish sculptress friend, Anne Marie Brodersen, about the arrival of a young Danish composer called Carl Nielsen: 'Nothing much for you, big eyes and a Copenhagenish humour.' But Anne Marie knew a little about him through a mutual friend, Margarethe Rosenberg, who taught music privately and had been at her parents' farm in south Jylland. She had also been at the première of the *Little Suite for Strings* at Tivoli in 1888.

They met on 2 March 1891 at a gathering given by the sculptor Stephan Sinding at his studio. Nielsen, always amusing company, entertained the guests, and Anne Marie sang some songs from her home district of Jylland. He was twenty-five and Anne Marie twenty-seven. Nielsen, who vaguely recalled having seen her on a train from Copenhagen, characteristically understated his account of their meeting in his diary: 'In the evening to a party ... Miss Brodersen is actually quite pretty. Got home at 2 o'clock.' The younger of their daughters would write a fuller account of this meeting in her memoirs: 'Father and mother met at the sculptor Stephan Sinding's studio on the Boulevard Arages, where father played a little for the guests. Mother was wearing a bright red dress and had brought her guitar. She sang Jylland dairy maid songs in a silvery voice, and she was very amusing. Father became infatuated with her and never took his eyes off her.'

Ambitious and headstrong, Anne Marie came from a strong, enterprising family. She was born on 21 June 1863 to Povl Julius Brodersen at Thygesminde, a large farm estate in the fertile part of south Jylland. Her father, who came from Højer, served in the German Dragoons then moved north of the border to south Jylland where he purchased one of the best farms in South Stenderup, near Kolding. There he married his housekeeper, Frederikke Johanne

Kirstine Gylling, who also came from Schleswig and was two years his junior. The Brodersens were among the first to import bulls and Oxford sheep to Denmark directly from England. They were successful, daring people. From her earliest years Anne Marie became involved in farming, fascinated by animals and fearless in her handling of them. She rose early and rode around the extensive lands and meadows which they owned near their farm. One of her most remarkable sculptures was to be *The Charging Bull*, inspired by an incident in her youth, when she skilfully dealt with a mad, raging bull; this illustrates well her strength of character.

The day after their meeting, Nielsen went to the studio where she was modelling a bust of the artist and sculptor, J. F. Willumsen. Willumsen was impatient and grumbling as a model, and Nielsen managed to amuse him by saying, 'Still your rage, Thor, and don't let the thunder roar!' Anne Marie was thus able to finish her work and the couple agreed to meet again. From then on they went everywhere together, to museums, concerts and cafés. On 20 March they considered themselves married without ceremony or licence, but they agreed to formalize their relationship as soon as their papers came from Denmark.

They were both living on scholarships which soon ran out. With sadness they left Paris, which Nielsen had found much more to his liking than Berlin and Dresden, and travelled to Italy together on the last leg of their journey. Their papers arrived from Denmark, and on Sunday 10 May 1891 a marriage ceremony was held in the English Church of St. Mark's in Florence. Many of their friends were able to be present and remembered their impressions of Anne Marie, with her long golden hair, dressed in a black silk gown, low-cut, with a border of little black ostrich feathers along the neckline. The wedding breakfast was held at a café.

Needing to avoid the more expensive hotels, the couple wandered through the backstreets of Florence in search of an affordable room. They grew tired of walking and continued by cab. Their cab driver was asked to stop outside a notice which read *Camera piano due* (second-floor room), whereupon Nielsen exclaimed, 'Ah, two pianos – that's for us.' (Throughout his musical career, Nielsen made extensive use of Italian terms, more often for their sonority than for their exact meaning.) The cab driver then demanded such an excessive sum that

Nielsen flew into a rage, frightening the driver so much that he ran away. For the rest of their honeymoon, lack of money was a serious problem for the newly-weds: they had adopted a stray dog and Anne Marie, used to a high standard of living, had proved to be very extravagant. They agreed that from then on Carl would look after their money.

It was time to go home. They arrived in Denmark married and penniless, to face two sets of shocked parents. The Brodersen family was the first to be visited. Nielsen was impressed by the grandeur of the Jylland farm manor and viewed it with some awe, but his father-in-law was offensive, referring to him as 'the fiddler boy from Fyn'. Nothing could distress the two young people, however: they were totally dedicated to their art and to each other. Brodersen's obstinate daughter had already rebelled by choosing to devote her life to an artistic career of which he had disapproved, and he is reputed to have told her: 'I will give neither my daughter nor my money to something which I believe will come to nothing.' And now he despised her for trusting herself to a mere fiddler boy from Fyn.

At the time of Nielsen's studies in Copenhagen he had an affair with the maid of the house he lived in, and a son, Carl August Hansen, was the result of their union. When Anne Marie married Carl she wished to adopt the boy but her husband seems to have been against this. (He did stay in touch with his son, however, who after an unsuccessful spell at the Copenhagen Conservatoire became a pharmacist and settled in New York.)

As soon as Anne Marie married Carl she was to have all the freedom she needed, working away from home for long periods in order to pursue her career. She had already opposed her father in studying sculpture, first at a school in Schleswig, and – with her mother relenting first – from 1882 as a private pupil of August Saabye in Copenhagen (as a woman, she had been refused by the leading Danish sculptor C. V. Bissen). In 1889 she was admitted to the Women's School of Art and in 1890 won the Academy Scholarship, enabling her to travel to Paris, France and Italy. Within a few years she began to exhibit regularly, winning major awards. She was a successful artist in her own right, especially noted for her equestrian and animal studies.

After visiting Nielsen's parents the newly-wed couple travelled to Copenhagen in June 1891 when Carl at last took up his employment

*Following page*, Thygesminde, the large farm estate in South Jylland where Anne Marie Brodersen was born

in the second violin section of the Royal Orchestra. They stayed in the 'Three Virgins', a hotel behind the Stock Exchange building, until they moved in October into a small backstreet attic flat, Nyhavn 5; there they stayed for a year, hardly noticing the cramped conditions until Anne Marie was expecting their first child. Their daughter was born there on 9 December and named Irmelin Johanne after J. P. Jacobsen's poem *Irmelin Rose* which Nielsen had set to music that year. As Christmas was approaching Anne Marie wanted to make a festive christening party for their artist friends but money was very tight. A cot was made and decorated in her favoured bright primary colours. Around this some heads of cabbage were arranged, with large candles burning inside them. In the centre lay the baby, surrounded by musicians all around her, clapping their hands. The flat was too small for all the guests to be able to squeeze into it at the same time and they had to take turns.

Soon after Irmelin's birth, Carl was left to look after her during the daytime while Anne Marie worked. After returning home from playing in the orchestra in the evening, he would work late into the night on the composition of a symphony, the biggest project he had yet conceived. Sketches for the work dated back to his stay in Berlin, and his inspiration had been Beethoven's Fifth Symphony, which he attempted to memorize. Composing his first symphony was not without difficulty – Nielsen had had very little experience of orchestral playing and other than the *Little Suite for Strings* he had only attempted a single movement for orchestra in 1888 (now known as the *Symphonic Rhapsody*). Added to this, the stamina required to sustain his creative work as well as private pupils, childcare, domestic chores and orchestral duties began to put Nielsen's health under great pressure. Nonetheless, in his tiny attic flat, fighting alongside all his other commitments, Nielsen's first symphony began to take shape.

4

Carl Nielsen as portrayed
in a poster design of 1899 by
Susette Holten

*A Danish composer had written a symphony of
which the allegro movement was styled* allegro
orgoglioso *(i.e., proudly). After the first
performance the composer was congratulated by
an elderly, cultured, and really intelligent lady
who had confessed that the first movement had
given her most delight because throughout it
she had clearly heard the organ-like character
the composer had wished to express.*

Carl Nielsen, *Living Music*, 1925

# The Early Works 1891–99

Jens Peter Jacobsen (1847–85), novelist and poet. Almost all of Nielsen's songs were set to Danish texts: his first two published collections were settings of poems and verses by Jacobsen.

It is Nielsen's symphonies for which he is today best known outside Denmark. Within his native land, however, he is arguably better known for his huge body of songs – almost 300 in total. These were varied, both popular and professional, for soloists and choirs, for church and theatre, and so encompassed a variety of objectives. Within these categories they evolved from formal Romantic Lieder to the freer styles and sonorities of twentieth-century chamber songs. His first songs, for soloist and piano, were written for recital purposes, and these early 'professional' songs should not be confused with his later songs which constituted his renewal of the Danish popular or folk song.

Nielsen's first two published song collections were published in 1892 and 1893; each was made up of five melodies, set to the verses of the contemporary Danish poet, Jens Peter Jacobsen, whose poem cycle Arnold Schoenberg set to music in his large-scale oratorio, *Gurrelieder* (1900–01). Of the first collection, *Genrebillede* ('A Genre Picture') was Romantic in style – a gentle pastiche with some archaic features; *Irmelin Rose* was straightforward as befitted its theme, 'All that is lovely', and was one of several works which bore a dedication to his wife. Four of the Five Songs were first performed on 28 April 1892 by Marie Nielsen (a commonly found name in Denmark) to an audience of about one hundred people. *Til Asali* ('To Asali') was not performed on this occasion as it was intended to be sung by a man. The Jacobsen songs are exotic and, although they mark only the beginning of Nielsen's departure from the Danish Romantic tradition that had preceded him, they were considered in his lifetime to be both difficult and different. 'Nielsen insists on composing differently from everyone else,' one critic complained, mentioning 'coarse harmonies and laboured modulations which stifle the effect'.

His third published collection of songs was composed to words by the young poet Ludvig Holstein in 1894, the same year that the poems had appeared as Holstein's debut. The composer was clearly well aware

Opposite, the first concert to feature only works by Carl Nielsen was held on 28 April 1892. The opus numbers given are erroneous; Nielsen cared little about such details.

Koncertpalæets mindre Sal.

Torsdag d. 28de April Kl. 8.　*1892*

# Carl Nielsen,

## Kompositions-Soirée.

*Program.*

1. *Strygekvartet i fmoll op. 6.*
   Allegro moderato ma energico.
   Un poco Adagio
   Allegretto scherzando.
   Allegro agitato
   D'Hrr. Kgl. Kapelmusici **Anton Svendsen, Holger Møller, Chr. Petersen og Frits Bendix.**

2. *Musik til fire Digte af I. P. Jacobsen.* (*Ny.*)
   Solnedgang.
   I Seraillets Have.
   Har Dagen sanket al sin Sorg.
   Irmelin Rose.
   Frøken **Marie Nielsen** og Hr. **Victor Bendix.**

3. *To Fantasistykker for Obo og Piano.*
   Romance.
   Allegretto.
   Fru **Orpholine Olsen,** født **Schram** og Hr. **G. Bruhn.**

4. *Strygekvintet i Gdur op. 4.*
   Allegro pastorale.
   Adagio.
   Allegretto.
   Allegro molto.
   D'Hrr. Kgl. Kapelmusici **Anton Svendsen, Holger Møller, Chr. Petersen, Osvald Poulsen** og **Frits Bendix.**

Flygel: *Hornung & Møller*

of contemporary Danish poetry. Whereas Jacobsen's poems had inspired Nielsen to write Lieder in the Danish Romance tradition of Peter Heise and Peter Lange-Müller, the songs written in 1894 marked a stylistic advance. Holstein's poems offer a more down-to-earth and less utopian portrayal of nature, to which Nielsen wrote strophic songs (repeating a single melody for successive verses of text, usually simple and lyrical in style).

They were first performed at a concert in Copenhagen on 3 February 1898 by Margarethe Boye and Ida Møller. The first notices denounced such beautiful songs as *Æbleblomst* ('Apple Blossom'), *Sommersang* ('The Summer Song'), and *Sang bag ploven* ('The Song Behind the Plough'), accusing Nielsen of 'a morbid craving for originality'. Another critic dismissed his work as 'neither song nor music but a random experiment with notes'. Many critics were clearly more at ease in the bygone age of Heise and Lange-Müller when texts were of a more romantic hue, and often other-worldly. The Holstein poems, particularly *Sang bag ploven*, however, concerned ordinary, working people. Although not actually intended as a popular song, *Sang bag ploven* was soon to be heard outside the concert hall and in its form, its pace of movement, its harmonic colouring, it anticipated the type of popular song which Nielsen would soon start to compose in earnest. Indeed, with *Sang bag ploven* the disparaging critics were listening to the future of the Danish song.

On 4 March 1893 Nielsen's second daughter was born and named after her mother, Anne Marie (Frederikke). Within the family, however, she was called *Søs*, that is, Sis[ter] (Nielsen had affectionately shortened her mother's name to Marie). She was born in the large, bright attic flat overlooking Ørsted Park, Nørrevoldgade 45, to which the family had recently moved. Many helpers had come to assist with the removal and Nielsen was confident that his piano could be negotiated up to the top floor. Unfortunately, the stairs were narrow and the piano slipped from their hands. Nielsen was able to wedge it against a wall, preventing it from falling downstairs, but the effort of this, combined with shock, precipitated the beginning of life-long heart trouble. He was in such pain that he had to be admitted to hospital. A further health problem developed into severe catarrh, for which Nielsen was put on a special diet and subjected to the extremely unpleasant treatment of a stomach pump.

But he never allowed physical ailments to block the creative process. His study trip of 1890–91 had acquainted him with many of Europe's leading musicians and the musical trends of the day. The journey had also broadened his awareness of literature and the visual arts. But perhaps most significantly, it had enabled him to resolve where he stood in the debate between those who saw the future of music in Wagner's vision, and those who saw it in the stricter, purer music of Brahms. Nielsen's point of departure as a composer undoubtedly lay in the latter, but he continued to admire Wagner's achievement. Of its limitations, as Nielsen saw it, he was to write some thirty years later:

> It is the taste, the Überschwängliche [rapturous, overripe, over-powering] and unwholesome, in Wagner's theme that is intolerable. The only cure for this sort of taste lies in studying the basic intervals. The glutted must be taught to regard a melodic third as a gift of God, a fourth as an experience, and a fifth as the supreme bliss. Reckless gorging under-mines the health. We thus see how necessary it is to preserve contact with the simple original.

Nielsen saw his choice of Brahms not as a return to the music of the past, but as a firm grasp of music's fundamental principles and thus of its future. Contrary to Wagner's vision, better progress could be made by a process of simplification rather than by an elaboration of what he believed had become adulterated by the late nineteenth century. In the String Quartet in F minor (No. 2), composed in 1890, he expressed a powerful torrent of fresh ideas within a chamber genre whose formal structure he had mastered; in 1888 he had written the *Little Suite for Strings* and an unpublished movement for symphony orchestra. Over this period he was fusing his mastery of form with an increasing predisposition towards orchestral music.

'Symphony No. 1,' Robert Simpson wrote in his influential book, *Carl Nielsen: Symphonist*, 'shows that Nielsen was already clear as to his real path as a composer, for it displays the principle of evolving tonality: indeed, it might not be going too far to say that it is probably the most highly organized first symphony ever written by a young

man of twenty-seven.' Sketches for the untitled symphony had begun
in Berlin in the autumn of 1890 while Nielsen was still finishing his
String Quartet. In his travel diary, he recorded on 20 December, 'I
have made a good start on the Finale ...' Six months later, he brought
the work home, and between domestic chores and orchestral duties
returned to the score in his attic flat. The completed symphony
was first performed on Wednesday 14 March 1894 at Copenhagen's
Theatre Royal, as part of the concert which opened the orchestra's
new self-financing scheme. Johan Svendsen conducted, and the
composer played at his usual place in the second violins. The audience
included Christian IX, Queen Louise and other members of the
Danish royal family.

The symphony attracted enthusiastic applause and Nielsen was
called to take a bow with the conductor three times. While Norway's
most celebrated composer, Edvard Grieg, wrote him a letter of congratulations, the influential Danish music critic, Charles Kjerulf,
began a lifelong conflict with Nielsen in the nation's principal daily,
*Politiken.* He described the symphony's music as 'unsettled and violent
in its harmonies and modulations ... as if one is witnessing a child
playing with dynamite'.

Nielsen's treatment of tonality was the symphony's most innovative
feature. He took a middle way, neither abandoning tonality nor
being restricted by its previous limitations, whereby all dissonance
necessitates resolution, all tension release. In his seminal study of
Nielsen's symphonies, Robert Simpson argues that the composer
developed a dynamic view of tonality, in that most of his mature
works treat a chosen key as a goal to be achieved. 'His final establishment of the key has all the organic inevitability and apparently
miraculous beauty with which the flower appears at a plant's point of
full growth.' Also called 'progressive tonality', this dynamic view of
tonality is defined with misleading simplicity in the Concise Oxford
Dictionary of Music as: 'Beginning a symphonic movement in one
key and ending it in another, as in certain works of Nielsen and
Mahler.' Opening the symphony, its designated key being G minor,
with a chord in the formally unrelated key of C major was not a ploy
of Nielsen's to *create* extra tension – instead it may be viewed as the
beginning of the aim to be achieved, the tension to be resolved. But
now Simpson's descriptions in the early 1950s of Nielsen's 'progressive'

or 'evolving' tonality have been displaced by more complex structural analyses, especially of the later symphonies. The issue of Nielsen's approach to tonality provides perennial material for scholarly dissertations which verbalize many patterns of the composer's intentions. Just as Wagner aims by a Leitmotive to give the unconscious mind a meaning, mood or association outside the music, so Nielsen's plateaux of tonality suggest abstract musical relationships, movement and patterns which emulate the dynamic flux of life. Many 'meanings', or none at all, may be attached to such music.

Whatever the music can be said to mean, Nielsen's First Symphony – which preceded the first symphonies of both Mahler and Sibelius – is a work which sums up the essence of the young composer, in so far as it is assertive, vigorous, independent and optimistic. Viewed next to the maturity and architectural mastery of Brahms's First Symphony (composed when he was forty-three), Nielsen's achievement at the comparatively young age of twenty-seven is bold and highly individual. It is so individualistic that its fingerprints incidentally disclose a self-portrait (the first movement is, after all, subtitled *proudly*). The slow movement unfolds in a deeply inspiring panorama; but unlike much Nordic music in which time seems to stand still, Nielsen's tempos are urgent. The 6/4 time signature of the third movement is more complex than that of the standard scherzo, and the finale, although in the tonic key of G minor, reflects the opening movement by beginning and ending firmly in C major. To use Robert Simpson's phrase, this is 'music which marches with a long athletic stride'.

Dedicated to Marie, the symphony was published in 1894 by Alfred Hansen in whose company Nielsen felt increasingly at ease. Despite the composer's convivial nature, Copenhagen seemed to alienate him: he was too down-to-earth for pretentious circles but too successful for the liking of his peer group. It created some resentment among them that a rank-and-file player in the second violins should have written a symphony which immediately attracted acclaim.

Travelling once more, in November 1894 Nielsen went alone to Berlin to arrange the performance of his symphony in Germany, and from there to Vienna with a score to present to Brahms, a man renowned for his severity. Nielsen arrived at Brahms's house with a

The Danish Royal Orchestra
with conductor Johan
Svendsen, photographed
c. 1894, the year the
orchestra gave the première
of Nielsen's First Symphony

mutual friend, Dr Schiff, who had accompanied the young composer to give him courage. The two men were led to Brahms's bedroom by a maid but he was not there. 'S. knocked on the next door, and a clear strong voice called "Come in,"' Nielsen wrote to Orla Rosenhoff.

> *I let Schiff go in alone and remained in the bedroom … when I heard Schiff mention my name I went in to join them. Brahms greeted me somewhat indifferently and bade me sit down. I sat myself down in the nearest chair which happened to be a rocking chair, and it swung me right back so that my legs were in the way. When I had found a more comfortable position, he began to talk with Dr Schiff about all sorts of things without taking the slightest notice of me. This suited me well, as I could thus observe him at my leisure and get an impression of him … Brahms is a medium-height, very stocky man, well-built and thoroughly thick-set, standing firm on his legs and giving the impression of having great strength. He is very short-necked and a little stooping if seen from behind … his back is rather round. His expression changes while he talks, and at times his eyes have a sarcastic, almost evil gleam, that soon changes into an expression of great cordiality and fondness … I had noticed that several times, while I was looking the other way, Brahms glanced at me sharply, as though scrutinizing me. Just what he thought of my reply, my appearance or anything, I simply do not know.*

Brahms asked if he might examine the Danish composer's work, although he said he would have to see him another time to discuss it. With that, he escorted Schiff and Nielsen 'right out to the street door, where he stood, broad and smiling on the threshold and waved at us'. A second meeting was not to take place, however, as Nielsen was not able to extend his stay in Vienna.

In the letter to Rosenhoff, Nielsen proudly related his reply to a tactless question of Brahms, 'And how is Thorvaldsen's Museum?', probably aimed at Nielsen in the belief that its meaning would be above his head. But Nielsen was well-aware of the meaning of this strange question and replied firmly, 'Oh yes, it's still there, Herr Doctor.' Most Danish musicians in fact knew the background to the Thorvaldsen comment, because Gade's daughter had spread the story. From 1866 to 1868 both Joachim and Brahms had performed at the

Johannes Brahms – Nielsen travelled to Vienna to present him with the score of his First Symphony.

Music Society in Copenhagen. Gade had hoped that art might help to erase memories of the war of 1864 and relied upon the tact of the German artists. Joachim never behaved in a provocative way and was well-received in Denmark. Brahms was a different matter, however. He had been a guest at Gade's home after a recital and began to praise the German victory and Bismarck's genius. This provoked tension and a toast to Bismarck's death, which Brahms countered by saying, 'We will discuss that when Thorvaldsen's Museum is standing in Berlin!' Berteo Thorvaldsen (1770–1844) was a neo-classical sculptor, and the first internationally acclaimed Danish artist.

Among papers found after Nielsen's death was a copy or draft of a letter in formal German addressed to Brahms but probably never sent. In this letter the master was repectfully urged to fulfil his offer to examine and comment on a few of Nielsen's scores. A few years later, Brahms did give a few words of appreciation of Nielsen's symphony – through the music critic William Behrend.

In 1896 Nielsen was invited to conduct his symphony in Dresden, and hoped that this would prove to be the turning point in his career. Aware of this, Marie wrote to him, 'If only I could be with you – you have conducted before, but have you had enough rehearsals? It's a foreign orchestra, you know, in a foreign country and language. I am very anxious about the reviews. Nováček, that devil, has led you astray enough and I suppose that you came to Dresden and went round like a poor fellow – my poor little man! Don't let him mislead you again when you are in Berlin. Remember me to Nováček and Busoni ... Hear as much music as you can, my dear, and tell us a little about contemporary literature in Germany.'

Her husband's detailed reply must have allayed her fears.

*The evening went really well ... and I had much success with the audience, as you may know from the telegram that was sent to Hansen for the benefit of the newspapers. But it was not the tremendous success that it was in Copenhagen. After the first movement, strong applause; after the Andante, so much strong applause that I had to appear before the audience three or four times to bow. After the third movement, three times and at the end I was called back most vigorously after the Finale ... again I find that there is so much life and movement in it that I think the piece really does possess some spark. The precise form and exact way of expression have, I hope, both surprised and impressed people here and I am certain that such a work will be able to achieve something good and open up the ears and eyes to all that German slavering and obesity that one finds among Wagner's imitators. Everyone here says that it was a* grosser, schöner Erfolg *[great, beautiful success] ... after the concert we were all together and in the end Alfred Hansen, Busoni, Nováček and I went around the town to all kinds of places and did not get home until 5 a.m. We were all very sober, so don't worry, my dear.*

The distinguished critic Georg Riemenschneider was greatly impressed. 'I must confess that I have never known a more remarkable work. The composer, who, until now, in spite of my great interest in the Nordic people, was quite unfamiliar, shows a characteristic that only rarely occurs and in recent years, simply not at all. The symphony is, from the first to the last note, outstandingly original, with no echoes of other people's works. Certain and sound, this sterling artist treads his own path.'

Nielsen's works for solo piano were also increasingly individualistic and were criticized because they did not develop from those of

Chopin and Liszt who 'thought with their fingers'. While he did not aim to recreate an orchestra through the keyboard, his next piece for solo piano, the *Symphonic Suite* of 1894, was the exception to the rule. In this work Nielsen skilfully mixed the orchestral and solo piano genres, thereby arming the critics who would categorize him as a symphonist. He had moved far from the captivating lightness of the Five Piano Pieces, completed only four years earlier. In a bold attempt to find a denser texture, in the *Symphonic Suite* Nielsen pianistically portrayed massive orchestral sonorities and long-sustained *ff-fff* dynamic levels.

The work was prefaced with a motto from Goethe: 'Ach, die zärtlichen Herzen! Ein Pfuscher vermag sie zu rühren.' ('Ah, those tender hearts! Any bungler can move them'). According to Christian Christiansen, the renowned Danish professor and pianist who became a close friend and colleague of Nielsen in his later years, the quotation only indicated the character of the composition and that the composer 'was aware that it was not pleasant either for the fingers or the ears'. By using this quote Nielsen made it clear that he was rejecting the sentimentality and bombast of the late nineteenth-century Romantic repertoire. He was also fusing elements of both symphony and suite; but although the *Symphonic Suite* contained traits of both forms, it lacked the dynamic structure that drives either of its namesakes.

The *Symphonic Suite* was published in 1895 with a dedication to the pianist, teacher and composer Victor Bendix. (A pupil of Liszt in Weimar, and the cousin of Emil B. Sachs, Bendix was one of Nielsen's earliest and most influential supporters.) It was first performed, with Louis Glass as soloist, on 5 May 1895 in Copenhagen. Some of Nielsen's songs were also in the programme for this concert arranged by the musical society Symphonia, but it was the piano piece which provoked the most controversy. Nielsen responded to the critical reviews with:

*I have already been obliged to hear a great deal, both good and bad, about this last work of mine and our very own Doctor of Music, Mr Hammerich, has told Mr Glass that the work was an insult to people, etc. The audience responded admirably to my music and both the* Suite *and the songs were a great success.* Politiken *today is unsympathetic towards*

Ferruccio Busoni (1866–1924), the Italian-born pianist and composer, met Nielsen in Berlin and the two became friends. He was to be the dedicatee of Nielsen's Second Symphony.

*me and calls the* Suite *'Music of the Will'. The other papers I haven't seen, but I expect nothing from any side and my hopes rest in the future alone.*

It was a major obstacle to the success of his piano music that the composer lacked the virtuosity to perform it himself. In Nielsen's opinion, Louis Glass had failed to grasp the spirit of the piece. Six years later, Kjerulf was still snarling in *Politiken* after a recital of the work by Dagmar Borup: 'She even had the courage to play two pieces from Carl Nielsen's almost notorious *Suite* ... but without managing to convince us that this is music.'

After six light pieces, the *Humoreske-Bagateller*, Nielsen would not attempt to write any major keyboard works for more than twenty years. Light-hearted and innocent in character, the bagatelles were composed over the years 1894–7, dedicated to his children, and first performed on 3 February 1898 by Johanne Stockmarr, who had studied with the composer. Most reviews were favourable, to the extent of finding nothing objectionable in the pieces, but one critic remarked that these tone portraits were aimed at 'children of thirty'. This perceptive comment was also an apt, but accidental, description of the composer at the time.

Nielsen's Sonata in A major for Violin and Piano had been completed on 23 August 1895. Violin and piano are treated as equal partners in this work (dedicated to the young French violinist, Henri Marteau): two fast movements are characterized by intense rhythmic and contrapuntal writing with melodic themes quickly dismissed or developed; the slow movement expresses intense feeling without being sentimental. The sonata was first performed on 15 January 1896 by Johanne Stockmarr and Anton Svendsen, leader of the Royal Orchestra, in Copenhagen's Concert Palace (now the Odd Fellow Hall).

It was not what Nielsen's public had anticipated, even though it employs a great deal of the dynamics of the composer's string quartets and symphony. The music was unconventional and the critics reacted accordingly: 'Strange and dislocated ... a futile experiment', according to Kjerulf, while in *Dannebrog* Robert Henriques wrote: 'Fear of not being sufficiently interesting diverts Mr Nielsen from natural paths,' and, 'The more lucid parts are mere repetitions of what the composer has already expressed on a number of occasions, and the remainder would appear to have arisen from mathematical combinations rather than from inspiration and feeling.' *Berlingske Aftenavis* feigned sympathy, but, 'with the best possible will ... it was impossible to understand the least bit of what the work had to say.' 'Perhaps,' suggested *Nationaltidende*, 'it is the preserve of future generations to discover anything beautiful and natural where we only find contrived oddities.'

Unperturbed by these negative responses, Nielsen told the Swedish composer Bror Beckman in February 1895: 'no one can hold a work back if it is good, and time alone will reveal judgement and skill.' To Nielsen, the kind of music which the critics admired had degenerated into 'effect-music', whereas he sought to express rather than idealize nature, including human nature, and this even extended to its more unappealing ugly parts.

Nielsen's son, Hans Børge, was born on 5 September 1895. In his youth the child contracted meningitis, suffering brain damage as a result; although he lived until 1956 he played no part in the affairs of his influential family. He appears in family photos but is scarcely mentioned in correspondence or diaries. References to Hans Børge in the Carl Nielsen Archive are often conspicuous by their absence, reflecting the social repressions and conformities of a bygone age.

Marie was selective in her own conformity. She spent much time away from home in pursuit of her career, and by 1896 Carl's reservations about these long absences emerge in correspondence, as does the extent of his loneliness. He wanted there to be a different balance between domestic and artistic priorities and on one occasion wrote to his wife: 'To hell with the stuff we create when it's at the expense of our children's happiness and welfare. That is now my opinion. I would rather look after little Hans Børge once than look one hundred times upon the best work of art.' In her memoirs, Søs recalled how her father would often play with them at their own level, noting that he never entirely lost the uninhibited innocence of childhood. His artistic and domestic obligations amounted to too heavy a workload, however, and he eventually advertised for a housekeeper. A stout lady from Fyn, Madame Jensen, was employed and stayed with the family for one year.

In the winter of 1896 Nielsen learned that his mother, Maren Kirsten, was very weak, and so he and Marie travelled to Fyn on 22 January 1897. Six days later Maren Kirsten died. So powerful had been her influence over the family that both Carl and his father Niels were deeply shaken. In a letter to Bror Beckman, Nielsen wrote the moving words:

*She had been my helper and friend for my whole life; I can say that without my dear mother I would have become nothing in this world. In spite of her poor conditions and many children, she never lost courage, but strongly urged us all to strive for the highest ideals in work and diligence. If I now become something in the world, my mother's name will shine even brighter, for there will never be another of her character. It's not easy*

Carl and Anne Marie Carl-
Nielsen with their children
(from left to right) Irmelin,
Anne Marie and Hans Børge

*for you to imagine my state at the moment. My father is still alive and is
in complete despair, so I have to look after him too.*

Both Carl and Marie disliked living in the city, but she had to
remind him of their dedication to their careers, and so dissuade him
from taking over her parents' farm at Thygesminde in the south of
Jylland (an option that was open to them). However, with her sister
Lucie, they kept on the manor house in which Nielsen occasionally
found peace to compose. While Marie was working on a relief of King
Frederik III and Queen Sophie Amalie on horseback for Copenhagen's
new town hall in the summer of 1897, tensions increased between
the married couple, and it was not just the city from which Nielsen
escaped when he arrived at Thygesminde, disturbed and unable to
work on his third string quartet. But on 2 August a letter of recon-
ciliation arrived from his wife. 'If you finish your finale, I shall work
hard on the horse and we shall never again spend a summer like
this year, my dearest ... we shall be good to each other and not put
pressures on one another so that we are unable to work.'

'Finished work on the first movement of a Quartet in E flat major
in December,' Nielsen noted in his diary, 'now working on the
Andante.' The exact date of the quartet's completion in 1898 is not
known, as the original score was lost. Nielsen had rolled up the
manuscript under his arm and set off through the city by bicycle. On
his way to the printers he saw a carriage whose horse had fallen and
asked a passing boy to hold the manuscript while he helped the
animal to its feet. When this was righted Nielsen turned to find that
the boy had gone, together with his manuscript, and neither boy
nor manuscript have ever been traced. The work was reconstructed
from a combination of Nielsen's sketches and memory, published in
1900 with a dedication to Edvard Grieg, and first performed in
Copenhagen on 4 October 1901.

The String Quartet No. 3, described by one of the critics as 'a
confusion of notes with neither meaning nor coherence', was not
immediately appreciated. A glimmer of light came from a sympathetic
musician who had been appointed to write for the *Illustreret Tidende*,
and who wrote on 24 November 1901: 'Here we have a young Danish
composer with a grasp of form and shaping comparable to that of
Johan Svendsen, and yet people are repelled by it. In one respect, of

course, this is understandable: when one is brought up on romances and romance-like music one loses one's responsiveness to more demanding material.'

By now the importance to Nordic music of Jean Sibelius in Finland and Carl Nielsen in Denmark was apparent to those with an eye to the future. The influence of the two composers dominated the development of Scandinavian music, although their styles differed too radically to support fully their well-established twinning. They were born in the same year, and their creative careers coincided almost exactly. From 1891–1925 both developed the twentieth-century symphony in national styles distinct from the hegemony of central Europe. Partly due to his impressive setting of unforgettable melodies and skilful use of the orchestral tone-palette of the nineteenth century, Sibelius was able to achieve an early popularity, whereas Nielsen, always concerned with the future of music, did not allow his listeners the safety of repeated, developed themes so beloved of the nineteenth century – his melodies and motives were concise. In 1901 Nielsen was granted a government stipend to support his work as a composer. Sibelius had already been endowed by a much smaller nation in 1897, and ten years later the Finn was granted a lifetime annuity while Nielsen was conducting the Danish Royal Orchestra for the same salary as an ordinary musician. He complained to Beckman in 1902:

*I am still with the Royal Orchestra and play my Second Violin with the greatest aversion. I haven't been promoted, either to leading Second Violin or Deputy First and have not even become a Professor, even though that is something which is almost impossible to avoid in this land. I hope that Our Lord will protect me from this for a few years yet, for I am certain that such a title would insult me to death.*

Nielsen suffered from a lack of assertiveness rather than a failure to appreciate his own worth. In a letter written the following month to a fellow-artist he respected, the Danish tenor Vilhelm Herold, he said, 'Is it not true that although one cannot, as an artist, dispense with the approval of the general public, it nevertheless goes without saying that it's really for the sake of mankind that one plays, sings, works, and acts?'

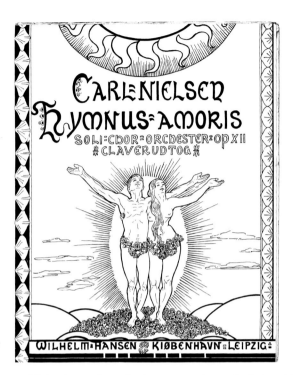

The cover of Nielsen's oratorio *Hymnus amoris*, first performed in April 1897 and published in 1898

Nielsen's experience in the opera orchestra had given him a preoccupation with music written on a larger scale. *Hymnus amoris*, an oratorio rather than an opera, was completed on 26 December 1896, but its inspiration came from years before, in Padua. Shortly after Carl and Marie's marriage, while travelling, the couple were deeply stirred by Titian's painting of a man stabbing his wife in jealousy. On the score of Nielsen's marvellous hymn to love he wrote: 'To my own Marie. This music is a pale reflection of reality, but if you ever hold me in your love, I shall strive to attain a higher expression of the supreme power of our lives. Then we two shall rise higher and higher towards our goal, and all our striving shall be love in life, as well as in art.'

Characteristically, Nielsen had allowed his idea to develop over a long time. He decided to express four aspects of love, each sung by different age groups. A choir of children sings, 'Love gives me my life/ It clothes me as I grow up', then young people with, 'Love is my hope and my desire/For me it shines like a star.' A male choir follows, singing 'Love is my spring/And valour grows on its banks' and during this section, a soprano solo interrupts to represent an unhappy woman: 'Love is my grief/Nothing has hurt me so much/Yet it is precious to me.' Finally, to represent old age, the massed choir sings, 'Love is my peace/Love is my sunset.'

The text was written in Danish by Axel Olrik, following an outline by Nielsen, who observed that it was so excellently written that Olrik deserved the great part of the honour, 'if there is any'. Nielsen's decision to use a Latin text, prepared from Olrik's Danish by the classical scholar J. L. Heiberg, provoked an adverse reaction from some staunch upholders of the Danish language. But Nielsen was unrepentant, stating that in Latin 'the words make a more objective and solid effect ... the text repetitions are not so disturbing in that tongue, and in fact one can sing much better in Latin on account of the numerous vowel sounds. See for example:

*Kærligheden giver mig livet (Love gives me life)*
*Amor mihi vitam donat*

*or again:*

*Kærligheden er min fred (Love is my peace)*
*Amor est pax*

*Do you see?*

While the Danish text was being translated into Latin, the composer studied Palestrina and other masters of vocal polyphony. He aimed for a universal style, neither modern nor derived from the nineteenth-century chorale. Nielsen achieved an intensity in *Hymnus amoris* without hysteria or sentimentality which, in the true manner of genius, appeared deceptively easy – until one reflects that the subject of love is at the very heart of the Romantic style which Nielsen considered too subjective. His hymn to love avoids personal feeling yet the work is still on a human rather than an epic scale. A single musical theme and a single movement in four sections unite the feeling of love as universal to the four ages of life.

The score, for soloists, four-part chorus, children's choir and orchestra, was dated 27 December 1896 and received its first performance on 27 April 1897 in Copenhagen, with Nielsen conducting. It immediately won Nielsen both critical and popular acclaim. The critics who maintained their hostility to Nielsen's music, including *Politiken*'s Kjerulf and *Dagbladet*'s Hammerich, were now themselves criticized. Robert Henriques, who began to write for *Dannebrog*, wrote an enthusiastic review and from then on took it upon himself to support Nielsen's music. The oratorio was also well received outside Denmark. Many years later, following a performance in Helsinki in

Carl Nielsen photographed at the time of his first successes as a composer

1921, the proud composer wrote home: 'They poured out to my carriage and wanted to touch my clothes. I think that in that moment I could have healed the sick.'

The theologian and musicologist Jørgen I. Jensen, whose study of Nielsen is in the context of his Danish culture, wrote that there 'is little doubt that Nielsen, in exploiting the sonorities of classical Latin and the polyphonic style, which together give the work a quasi-ecclesiastical character, had the ambition of creating a vision of a new church of art and love, expressed for instance at the end, when the choir sings not A-MEN but A-MOR ... This elevated notion of love was very much in sympathy with the then-current Symbolist movement.'

There can be little disputing the fact that Nielsen's humanism parallels the religious establishment and rituals he would never embrace.

*5*

Nielsen conducting his comic opera *Maskarade*; this cartoon appeared in the Danish newspaper *Politiken*, 1906.

*A few composers have written their own texts; but though Wagner's example may be tempting, it is hardly one to be followed. For when a composer writes his own words, he will recoil, unconsciously, instinctively, from what may cause him trouble as a composer ... The composer should come fresh to his text, accepting both the inspiration and the difficulties which the author's words present.*

Carl Nielsen, *Living Music*, 1925

# **Operatic Ambitions** 1900–06

Nielsen was acutely aware that his creative career coincided with the dawn of modern art, invention and free thinking. He read the emerging works of Sigmund Freud but disparaged *The Interpretation of Dreams* (1899) which controversially analysed complex strata of the unconscious mind. Nielsen formed his own opinion of peoples' differences and similarities; his fundamental humanism continued even in the age of Freud to inform his views and creative process.

Human moods and characteristics were directly depicted in Nielsen's key works of the opening years of the twentieth century; because of this keen interest in musical characterization the works of this period, such as his opera *Saul og David* ('Saul and David') and his Second Symphony, have sometimes been described as belonging to his 'psychological period'. (Some later works, written between 1922 and 1928, were to invest woodwind instruments with a 'soul' or personality but these compositions differed radically in method and objective from the works of Nielsen's 'psychological' phase.) He continued to eschew sentimentality and emotional outpourings, however, and the debate on whether or not his music was a reaction against Romanticism continued. At this time Nielsen's art came the closest it ever did to programme music, with its basis on extra-musical ideas which are evoked through sound; but his preference then, as it would always be, was for music to be perceived more openly, to be free from any external meanings.

In complete contrast to his larger-scale symphonic and operatic works, and while writing them, Nielsen had the gift of being able to write concise yet poignant melodies and from 1899 he was constantly invited to do so by schools and choirs. *Græshoppen* ('The Grasshopper'), for two-part choir, which was composed for *J. Mikkelsen's School Songs*, was particularly popular. (Nielsen's daughters were playfully nicknamed 'the grasshoppers' by their schoolmates on account of this song.) Just before Christmas 1899 he wrote *Edderkoppens Sang* ('The Spider's Song') from the Danish poet

Adam Oehlenschlæger's *Aladdin* – Oehlenschlæger's story derived
from the Arabian Nights would later play a far bigger role in
Nielsen's œuvre.

In 1899 the Nielsen family moved to Toldbodvej 6, a block built
around a yard, originally hussar barracks. This home became a
familiar meeting place for a constant stream of artists. Many became
close friends of the family and lively evening gatherings after
concerts were frequent events. 'After such concerts there were great
celebrations,' Søs noted in her memoirs, '... wine flowed, food
was carried in and out and the whole house was radiant with festivity.'

During the years 1899–1901, as Nielsen worked on *Saul og
David*, his Copenhagen household became dominated by the epic

The cover to the score of
*Saul og David*, Nielsen's
opera of 1902; the score
was published two years
later.

confrontation between Philistines and Israelites. Neither Nielsen nor
his librettist seemed to have been aware of the previous failures at
the subject, which included an abandoned attempt some forty years
earlier in Denmark by J. P. E. Hartmann, based on a text by Hans
Christian Andersen. Nielsen's idea for the subject was not to portray
events but instead a nation's destiny shifting through the personalities
of two contrasting leaders: David, the joyful, courageous, trusting,
youthful and obedient servant of the Lord; and Saul, haughty, impuls-
ive and gloomy – prepared even to curse the Lord.

*Saul og David* was scarcely influenced by the lush operatic style
of Verdi which was then very much in vogue. Nielsen was already
forging a very individual idiom which was muscular, lively, concisely
melodic, contrapuntal and tonally free-thinking. After an intensive
study of Gregorian chant and Palestrina, Nielsen used his massed
choirs more as in an oratorio: this suited his Old Testament subject
because the chorus remains detached, other-worldly and impartial.
Even when it proclaims the voice of the people, it remains the voice of
destiny. It is neither a person nor a participator in the events. Nielsen's
stated aim was to compose a 'timeless' opera, the strength and lasting
power of which would be based on the very roots of Western music
rather than on its recent blossoms. In his search for a new operatic
style, Nielsen's use of the choir, a certain Scandinavian sound and the
musical depiction of moods and personalities represented an innovative step away from the opera of central and southern Europe. All
composers of opera at this time lived in the shadow of Wagner but
only a few could find a new method of characterization and integra-
tion of the plot. Nielsen did not like the way Wagner spoon-fed the
audience: 'each time a name is merely mentioned, one is invariably
served up with the Leitmotive of the person concerned, even if he has
been long dead and buried. I find it extremely naïve.'

Precisely when and how Nielsen decided on the subject for his first
opera is uncertain, but in a letter to his wife from Berlin dated
16 October 1894 he wrote: 'I saw a picture by a painter I have never
heard of before, namely Piero del Pollaiuolo. It is a David who has
slain Goliath. The composition is as simple as could be. David stands
up straight, legs parted with one hand at his side, rather like Verrochio's
well-known bronze statue. His attitude is youthful, bold and
victorious.' Nielsen's opera concerned a leadership conflict within a

kingdom that might be taken to reflect Denmark's own situation after the 1864 war. A unifying spirit of nationalism is split in the choral passages when the people sing, 'Saul has slain thousands, David tens of thousands,' the echoes of which are heard in Saul's troubled mind. Nielsen may have sympathized with David, but Saul – not denounced by the composer – remains the central character of the drama. By 1896 Nielsen was working out the struggle between the two contrasting personalities, developing the art of musical caricature with considerable subtlety. The 'great and strange' subject stirred and haunted him to such an extent that for long periods he could not free himself of it no matter where he was, even when sitting in the orchestra with his violin, busy with ballets and vaudevilles.

In September 1898 his plan for the opera was handed to his librettist Einar Christiansen, who finished the libretto in January 1899. Its major literary source is the First Book of Samuel; also included are some episodes from the Second Book of Samuel and some from Chronicles; in general the libretto adheres very closely to the biblical account, but certain events were fused in order to heighten dramatic intensity and others invented, such as a beautiful romantic encounter between David and Saul's daughter, Michal.

Background details surrounding the composition of the opera are not known. There was no correspondence between composer and librettist because they both lived in Copenhagen, but it is known that they were initially friends. A rift between them must have occurred at some point, however, as the composer's name is conspicuously absent from Christiansen's autobiography – and three days before Nielsen conducted the opera's première and the scores went on sale, Christiansen's text was independently published with the prefatory note, 'Naervaerende Tekst er forfattet i Januar 1899' ('this text was written in January 1899'), an act surely made to indicate his claim of priority. Life was imitating art: Nielsen was the young and trusting man, but a man of action; Christiansen remained aloof, suspicious and superior. It seems that tensions rooted in the latter's conceit erupted when it was the younger man, whom Christiansen viewed as something of an upstart, who received the acclaim for the opera. In every other respect, Einar Christiansen was the perfect choice for a librettist. He had been editor of *Illustreret Tidende*, a playwright and novelist. He had contributed texts for Danish operas by Rung, Tofft

A photograph from the first production of *Saul og David*, on 28 November 1902. In spite of the enthusiasm of the audience at the première, this first production received only two performances.

and Lange-Müller. He translated singing versions of many librettos. He was a competent pianist and had been a pupil of Rosenhoff. The existing tension between Nielsen and Christiansen was to increase when the latter was appointed director of the Theatre Royal in 1899.

Had Nielsen been a closet symphonist in every genre (as has been claimed), he would have begun the opera with a full overture. Instead he plunges immediately into the tension leading up to the battle with the Philistines. The king is furious to see his military advantage dissipating while he is forced to await the ritual blessing of the Lord's prophet, Samuel. Saul, although wholly devoted to his peoples' struggle, displays an independence of mind he knows is unacceptable in a theocracy. 'The Lord is evil, and evil am I because he has made me!' Samuel, arriving after a long delay, is portrayed with grave dignity. Furious at Saul's initiative, he declares: 'This day the Lord has rent the kingdom from you.' David, the shepherd boy who plays the harp at local functions, is called in to soothe the king. David befriends the king's son, Jonathan, and begins a relationship with the king's beautiful daughter.

In Act II David learns of the giant Goliath's offer to settle the tribal conflict by personal combat. David volunteers and Michal cannot hold him back. On his safe and successful return joy is unrestrained, but internal strife ensues, and David narrowly avoids Saul's spear. Act III begins with a calm orchestral prelude which is often performed independently as a concert piece. Under an open moonlit sky at the foot of the Hachilah Hill, Saul's warriors are searching for David. Samuel arrives and provokes Saul by reminding him that David is now anointed. In the resulting turmoil Jonathan is in despair and Michal runs off with David for safety.

Act IV concludes the drama. Israel and her divided rulers are faced with the threat of extinction. Saul, heavily disguised, sets out to the Witch of Endor to summon the spirit of Samuel, who chillingly predicts the king's grief and downfall. Set to powerful martial music, the battle goes badly as prophesied and Jonathan is found dead. Saul is in despair and in his final transgression of Mosaic Law takes his own life. The news reaches David and Michal who are overawed and the drama ends piously with a musical 'glory to God', the chorus declaring that Israel's hopes reside in David and that he 'shall found God's promised kingdom on earth'.

As the date of the opera's première drew near – 28 November 1902 – Nielsen's household was overwhelmed by rehearsals. Musical scores and drawings gave way to costumes, scenery, singers and the real-life feuds behind the presentations of dramas. During rehearsals Rudolph Simonsen (who sang the part of Saul) lost control and in a fit of jealousy towards Vilhelm Herold (singing David) he let go his spear; luckily it only tore some scenery. Nielsen frequently had to soothe and reconcile both singers and theatre management. In spite of all these difficulties, the opening night went very well and Nielsen was able to encourage each singer to find the greatest meaning in each role. The Danish tenor, Vilhelm Herold, was already Nielsen's friend; through this opera some of the musicians who had not previously cared for Nielsen's music became devoted admirers. A celebratory party after the successful first performance took place at Nielsen's home. Later, he wrote to his wife who was working in Athens:

Saul og David *went splendidly with the house quite sold out yesterday. In fact the house had sold out by 1 p.m. with many seats at double and higher prices. The audience were very enthusiastic and after the last act they would not leave until the lights were put out and the safety curtain lowered! The newspapers are furious and will allow me neither talent, heart, nor taste. Now I shall go forward with my work, for I know what I can do.*

Despite the success of *Saul og David* the theatre wanted to stage other works. Nielsen felt stifled by his regular duties and humiliated by the management. Although he deputized as conductor and had proved himself as a composer he was still relegated to being a mere orchestral musician. He poured out his desolation in a stream of letters to Marie. 'You asked about *Saul og David*. There were only two performances. The theatre could earn 2,000 DKr more with *Pagliacci* and Herold than with my opera, so I gave in and let it be laid aside for maybe the next twenty years ... I beg you not to mention my opera again, it hurts ...'

Nielsen put his disappointment aside and turned his thoughts to his second symphony. He had found its inspiration in a naïve woodcut he saw on the wall of a village inn on Sjælland. Each of its parts caricatured the four 'humours' believed in the Middle Ages to govern one's physical and mental characteristics. The images became an obsession with Nielsen and eventually suggested the basis of a four-movement symphony. This work, entitled *De fire temperamenter* ('The Four Temperaments'), which Nielsen began in 1901 while finishing *Saul og David*, received its première on 1 December 1902. His First Symphony, despite its debt to convention, was almost aggressively individual. The next was less assertive and more conventional in structure than its predecessor, but, following the first by ten years, showed Nielsen's greater technical assurance and presented engaging and witty portraits of the four characters. Nielsen published a short programme note with the music (expanded in 1931 into a longer and more elaborate description), but he generally preferred music to be absolute, free from external influences; if he did compose music on the inspiration of external events, art or literature, he kept the details to himself. Only in the following year, 1903, with the overture *Helios*, did Nielsen write actual 'programme music' (following ideas or plots as did the tone poems of Sibelius and Richard Strauss). *De fire temperamenter* was not a tone poem but a symphony, classically structured in four movements. Each movement portrays cycles of moods within a credible person, rather than adhering exclusively to each state of mind named. Although the listener need not identify all the psychological analogies, Nielsen commented that:

> *The four movements of the symphony are built on the concept of the four human character types: the impetuous (*Allegro collerico*), the indolent (*Allegro flemmatico*), the melancholy (*Andante malincolico*), and the cheerful or naïve (*Allegro sanguino*). But the impetuous man can have his milder moments, the melancholy man his impetuous or brighter ones, and the boisterous, cheerful man can become a little contemplative, even quite serious – but only for a little while. The lazy, indolent man, on the other hand, only emerges from his phlegmatic state with the greatest of difficulty, so this movement is both brief (he can't be bothered) and uniform in its progress.*

The work was completed exactly one week before the first night of *Saul og David* and was given its première only three days later. The composer conducted both works. His friend Henrik Knudsen transcribed the symphony for a four-hand piano version and together they took it to the renowned Italian–German composer Ferruccio Busoni in Berlin. The following year the symphony was published with a dedication to Busoni, who arranged to have the symphony performed in Berlin. And there, in 1903, Nielsen conducted its famous Philharmonic Orchestra in his most recent work. In Denmark, the audience had been enthusiastic but the press antagonistic. In Germany, the applause was merely polite and the press still antagonistic. In *Der Tag*, a Professor Krebs suggested that the composer should consult a music teacher who would advise him to learn first how to write a purer music. This comment naturally provoked controversy in the press, but was significantly countered by the suggestion that the composer of *Hymnus amoris* deserved the benefit of more considered criticism. After Berlin the symphony was performed in an all-Nielsen concert in 1905 in Copenhagen, then in various cities in Germany and Denmark.

But first Nielsen was to spend some time in Greece. Marie had chosen to spend an Ancker Scholarship in Greece, studying classical art. Her husband had earned some money from his opera, and having secured an annual contract with his publisher, decided to accompany his wife, leaving his affairs in the hands of his close friend and neighbour, Svend Godske-Nielsen. On 2 February 1903, just before leaving with Marie, Nielsen engaged Maren Hansen as housekeeper. She came from Ellinge, a village near Nyborg, and remembered the composer from his time as the grocer's assistant. Until her death in 1946, she was to keep house for the family with exceptional devotion, regarding it as her mission to do everything possible for the Nielsen children and to cater to the needs of their artistic parents. It was she who prevented children and visitors from interrupting their work. According to Søs, 'with Maren came the finest and most devoted heart that ever helped in a home.'

In Athens the two artists were treated as celebrities and the Conservatoire there provided Nielsen with a room overlooking the Acropolis; he had the use of a piano and everything else that he needed. He walked in the mountains, toured the art galleries and was impressed by the Acropolis. His celebrity status guaranteed gossip and the newspapers reported his every move, which included some

Maren Hansen, the Nielsens' devoted housekeeper, 'the finest and most devoted heart'

frivolous escapades: after Nielsen had spent a day hillwalking with a
Kapellmeister named Kremser, the latter boasted in a café how he and
Nielsen had had no matches on them and so he had complied
with the reckless Dane's idea to fire a pistol at the tip of his cigarette;
another amusing anecdote from this time concerned the arrest of
Nielsen and a companion by Turkish soliders for having walked
through the grounds of a fortress on a visit to Constantinople. When
the visiting celebrity established his identity, he and his friend were
released with effusive apologies. And on 8 April King George I of
Greece, who was Danish-born, invited Nielsen to a banquet; there
Nielsen learned that it was impolite to tell a reigning monarch, even
after the privilege of a long chat together, that he now had to leave
the party.

The *Helios Overture*, written in Greece, was Nielsen's only
composition in 1903, a slackness for which he chastised himself.
A poem written by Nielsen expresses the work's programme,
each line of which depicts a section of the orchestral overture:

*Silence and darkness*
*The sun rises with a joyous song of praise*
*It wanders on its golden way*
*And sinks quietly into the sea*

The treatment of the subject belongs to Nielsen's 'psychological'
style, as the sunrise is expressed not in any nature–realistic manner but
through the feelings it inspires – namely the sense of exhilaration
experienced at witnessing the rising sun, an object of veneration of
primitive man. The tempo quickens in an expression of the ecstasy
and joy felt by the sun-worshippers (Nielsen believed there was some
residue of the practice in Norway); slow music throughout would
have been a literal representation of the sun's measured traverse across
the sky rather than the human perception of the event.

As the orchestra in Athens was well-funded but not well-
established, Nielsen decided to take the score home to Denmark for
its first performance, which was given on 8 October. Once again, the
critic Kjerulf made a strong attack on Nielsen's work, and provoked
vigorous debate in Copenhagen's musical circle. Nielsen wrote to
Knudsen in Vienna: '... but you can't imagine how little it has affected

me, but the performance, naturally, suffered a great deal. On the other hand I have only allowed myself to be very slightly annoyed, in fact even less than usual, by what the papers write. I hardly feel that it concerns me, and I experience neither disgust nor contempt ...'

While in Greece, Nielsen sent a long letter in response to more antagonism, this time from a friend, the organist and composer Thomas Laub. He clearly recognized Nielsen's genius, a fact which merely intensified his loathing for his avant-garde music and his fear of its insidious threat to order and beauty. Nielsen valued Laub's friendship and opinions enough to make a considered response to the latter's sustained attacks. 'What is it that you really want? ... a music that is consciously archaic and simple and cuts off sinews and muscles every time they reveal a sign of excitement in life or passion? ... It is possible you are right in your judgement of my music, but *I* cannot believe that, for then my existence would be of no use to the world and so I should never set pen to paper again ...'

The only thing that Nielsen allowed to come before his work was his family. In 1904, Marie's mother died but the sculptress had to set her grief aside, as she was committed to completing one of her most remarkable and lasting achievements – the ornamentation and reliefs for the huge bronze doors of the Cathedral at Ribe (a town in southwest Jylland ten miles south of Esbjerg). There was a last-minute rush to finish the work before the consecration of the cathedral on 7 August. In her memoirs, Søs explained the images on the bronze doors:

*The whole family had acted as models. There are five reliefs in the form of a cross. On the middle relief, Christ is seen riding into Jerusalem upon an ass. As Christ, mother had used the painter Niels Skovgaard for a model. To the left of this one sees the crowds praising Christ. There stands my father holding up a palm leaf and calling out together with my brother as a boy. Nearby one can see Maren ... To the right is my sister, leading the procession with a palm. She is also to be seen flying as an angel upon the door-handle. I myself was used as an apostle symbol as an angel, but it's an angry angel.*

At the start of the musical season Nielsen returned to Denmark. Marie, the pattern of her independent career by now well established,

An informal photograph of
the Nielsen family at their
home in Toldbodvej in 1904;
from left to right, Hans
Børge, Anne Marie (Søs),
Carl Nielsen, Irmelin and
Anne Marie Carl-Nielsen

stayed on in Greece. During her long absences at this time and in the future, her husband had to be totally committed to his musical career, while acting as both father and mother. He remained devoted to his children, but never accepted Marie's career taking precedence over their marriage. Left by himself for long periods, he often found the need and opportunity for female companionship. That Nielsen was unfaithful to his wife has always been implicit knowledge in Denmark, but at the request of Nielsen's daughters, this whole area of his life is taboo and has seriously restricted biographical research.

Of Nielsen's ten commissioned cantatas, only his later work *Fynsk foraar* ('Springtime on Fyn') of 1921 was to achieve lasting popularity. *Søvnen* ('The Sleep'), begun in November 1903, was to a text by the Danish poet Johannes Jørgensen, whom Nielsen had approached. The composer, who could never be accused of resting on his laurels or of plundering old ideas of material, had made considerable strides in his technique since *Hymnus amoris*. The distressing nightmare scene, which follows *Søvnen*'s calm opening, is in fact one of the first expressive uses of dissonance to enter twentieth-century music: it anticipates by ten years Igor Stravinsky's *Rite of Spring* which, in 1913, marked the eventual turning point away from the supremacy of tonality, based as it is on the tension between diatonicism and chromaticism. Nielsen was disturbed by music which permitted audiences to sleep during musical performances, and so it was typical that he should express both aspects of sleep – the alarming as well as the refreshing. He portrayed, perhaps ominously, this darker side of the human predicament ten years before World War I:

*A pang – a burden ... Help me! Am I awake?*
*I'm threatened, hunted ... Something from me taken*
*I've lost my way – forever doomed to stray*

From the spring of 1904 Nielsen had been busy conducting all concerts given in the Theatre Royal in the absence of Rung and Svendsen's ill-health. But he was able to write to his wife:

*... I have now had two rehearsals of* Søvnen *... I consider it to be my most remarkable and most consummate work so far and I think that I have succeeded in expressing what I wanted. If Thorvaldsen was right*

*when he said that one is on the decline when one is proud of one's own work, then I shall be rich and vigorous in my decline, for I must admit that I love my* Søvnen *when I hear the tumult of its many voices in my ears ... Thorvaldsen's words are only true when they apply to artists who are not constant in their search for new and varied tasks and with me that is just as great a necessity as salt and sugar.*

Nielsen must have anticipated the critics' discomfort with this work: the dissonant effects portraying the nightmare in the cantata's central section were guaranteed to provoke critics who still basked in the serenity of the nineteenth century. At its first performance, conducted by the composer on 21 March 1905, Nielsen's portrayal of the grotesque was considered by even some of his admirers to be grotesque (especially as his music was mostly cheerful and positive). 'This ride,' wrote one critic, 'is literally speaking, the wildest chase of the falsest notes ... even the staunchest supporter of Danish music is on the verge of withdrawing all allegiance from Carl Nielsen.'

While the cantata's central section has always attracted undue attention for its novelty, the first section represents as great a departure from tradition, both in its musical mood and musical language. If *Søvnen* had been written by an acclaimed central-European composer, it might have been hailed as the masterpiece that ushered in twentieth-century music (its modern sonorities predated Stravinsky or Bartók by almost ten years). Instead, the critics in Copenhagen shunned its strange tonal trajectory which was dissonant and unpredictable compared with tonality's traditional orbiting of the home key.

Other European writers and artists had also started to herald the end of the joyous *fin de siècle*. Wagner in *Tristan und Isolde* (1865) had taken chromaticism as far as it could go; the work was the final impetus towards the twentieth-century's division of the octave into twelve equal intervals. With the traditional consonance–dissonance axis removed, how were composers to treat total dissonance as other than a cessation of music? Stravinsky had found a solution to the musical dilemma of dissonance by combining it with striking asymmetrical rhythm, Nielsen had earlier resolved the problem of dissonance through his rhythmic 'current', but the Copenhagen critics, who did not accept the future of music as depicted by Nielsen,

lacked the confidence of their more cosmopolitan colleagues who
considered Stravinsky with more understanding.

After finishing *Søvnen*, Nielsen's gloom delayed a start on his next
work, the comic opera *Maskarade*. Since 8 April 1904 he had continuously deputized as conductor at the Royal Theatre – and the
management had showed Nielsen some gratitude by allowing him
time off to compose. But over the year resentments had been building
up against Nielsen, who wished to be given the post of conductor
officially. Conditions were anything but harmonious. Chief conductor
Svendsen, once greatly admired by Nielsen, was approaching retirement. His successor Frederik Rung, a conscientious but unin-
spiring conductor, felt threatened by Nielsen. The director, Einar
Christiansen, the librettist for *Saul og David*, was officious and empty
in his promises to appoint Nielsen conductor, and had even accused
the composer in February 1905 of being unfit to take on public office.
The theatre's president, the Count, was dismissed by Nielsen as a
'harmless idiot'.

At the beginning of 1905 Nielsen considered moving to Germany
to make a fresh start if his wife's capital and income were enough for
her to provide for herself and their children for an interval. On

The Royal Orchestra's
farewell party for Carl
Nielsen, in March 1905,
commemorated sixteen
years of service in
the orchestra.

11 February he wrote to her: 'The envy and opposition that I have experienced at the theatre – certainly first and foremost from the two conductors – has quietly reached a point that today I tendered my resignation ... They have ... demanded that I should either play violin in the orchestra like a harmless common soldier and be their subordinate or that I should leave. So now this has happened and I am once more an idle man in the street.' Marie was sorely missed: she was the only person who could tell him, in his view, what was right for him and who could strengthen him in the way he needed. The correspondence between them at the time reveals that she was similarly worried about set-backs in her own career.

On 21 February 1905 Nielsen expressed his feelings of anger and disappointment to his friend Klaus Berntsen, one of the patrons who had arranged his entrance to the Conservatoire, and who now served on the board of the Theatre Royal. Nielsen felt that Christiansen had no basis for saying he was unsuitable for a post in public life, and to Berntsen related at length his unblemished career as soldier, student, then theatre employee. To cap it all, when the composer had asked Christiansen whether he had a basis for such criticism, the latter said he had none.

Three weeks after writing to Berntsen, Nielsen was informed of the theatre's decision that in the following season he would continue as a member of the second violins only. His opponents had triumphed. He needed, admittedly, both the salary and to maintain vital links with the Danish national theatre, but felt that this position was unacceptable. Unable to consult his wife, Nielsen on 21 March 1905 decided on his own to tender his official resignation from the orchestra in which he had served for sixteen years.

That autumn he was confined to bed with heart trouble, diagnosed as a lack of blood supply to the heart muscles. Marie felt obliged to return from Greece for a month to comfort him. The rift with the theatre combined with this illness made him understandably very depressed but once he recovered, the 'undercurrent', to use Nielsen's own term, took over and he returned to writing his comic opera *Maskarade* with a speed which took even him by surprise. Despite the theatre troubles earlier in the year, initial progress had been good. 'I am now well on the way with *Maskarade*, indeed I think that I have never before worked so swiftly and easily. I experienced strong birth pangs before I was able to activate myself into the theme and atmosphere,' and he wrote on 18 February 'Sometimes I have a strange feeling that I am simply not myself, Carl August Nielsen, but merely an open tube through which there flows a stream of music, like mild and strong impulses vibrating in a kind of blissful motion. Then it's joyous to be a composer, you may be sure.'

*Maskarade*, a comic exposé of social mores, rigorous conventions and riotous behaviour, was different to anything Nielsen had previously written, and it proved the composer's versatility. Brimming with humour and invention, the music had the masterful touch of a modern Mozart (especially considering the speed of its composition). In 1904 Nielsen had borrowed an edition of Mozart's letters, the composer's music and personality having always been especially dear to him. Two years later he was to write a remarkable essay, 'Mozart and Our Time', in which he identified and compared two artistic temperaments, the severe and intellectual, next to the light-hearted and smiling. Mozart he clearly viewed in the latter category. This essay provides a rare glimpse into Nielsen's largely unwritten theory of music. On the question of whether it is possible to have a revolution in music, as in politics, he concluded that it is not. 'It is the great merit of the spiritual life that it can preserve continuity and cannot be killed by circumstance.' Nielsen's famous denial of the possibility of revolution in art reveals the limits he placed on his own search for originality. While he appeared to many of his Danish contemporaries as the instigator of a musical *coup d'état*, he distinguished between music's fundamental principles and later more ephemeral growths or flowerings, seeing his own originality not as a revolution, but as a return to fundamental principles. 'It is as if there are two levels to him [Mozart]. His moods alternate rapidly, like the colours refracted from a prism, now illuminating, now eclipsing one another. When he smiles it is often with tears in his eyes ...' Nielsen commented on the generative power arising from this perfect balance in Mozart's music, which – to quote Goethe – is then passed from generation to generation. Although Nielsen's music is not readily compared to Mozart's, this discussion of the effect of his illustrious predecessor's music may be taken as comments upon his own music.

Any parallels between the two composers are most often drawn when the *buffo Maskarade* is discussed. The idea of basing its libretto on Holberg's play of 1724, *Mascarade*, had occurred to Nielsen early in 1904 when he sketched out a plot which he passed to the literary historian and Holberg specialist Vilhelm Andersen. A furious uproar arose among certain literary people who objected that no one should touch a play written by the revered playwright Ludvig Holberg (1684–1754), the so-called 'Molière of the North'. Explaining his choice of subject in *Politiken* of 15 October 1905, Nielsen said: 'If anything, it was the Intermezzo, the element of masque comedy, that interested me, I think. And then Henrik in *Mascarade*. I think he is great ... he is quite modern in his feelings after all: he even says socialist things.'

Nielsen issued a statement to defend the desecration he was supposedly about to commit with Vilhelm Andersen. 'If it had concerned one of the character comedies, I would have considered the objections legitimate myself, but here, you see, we have one of Holberg's most obvious masque comedies.' Nielsen's choice of the librettist was a man whom he met in an amateur drama and instantly liked. It was a good choice. Andersen was a distinguished scholar, well versed in Danish literature as well as Greek and Latin. But he was no dull academic as his colourful, risqué and explicit dialogue proves. On the occasion of the 100th performance of the opera on 18 March 1946, Andersen recalled his meeting with Nielsen: 'Suddenly he stood in my room. I can see him before me today. I did not know him then, and I think I had scarcely heard of him, but he was very keen and tried in every possible way to persuade me to set to work on the venture.' Both men agreed on the plot and Andersen prepared the libretto in April and May 1904.

*Maskarade* was a complete contrast to *Saul og David*. Unlike the earlier dramatic opera, the comic opera was based on plot rather than characterization. The action is set in Copenhagen in the spring of 1723 when the frivolities of the masquerade, the masked ball, had become an issue of political concern on account of its alleged indecency. At Holberg's ball two young people betrothed to each other both meet and fall in love with masked partners. Their respective families, concerned with maintaining appearances of dignity, fear breaches of promise and scandal. Plots are hatched and go awry. The crisis is only resolved when the two young people discover that the objects of their infatuation at the ball are none other than each other. The opera mocks the pretentiousness of a polite urban society – especially the affairs and transactions of the establishment figures with whom Nielsen had never felt comfortable. (This social critique, underlying an otherwise light-hearted comedy, is biographically revealing. Two letters written by Nielsen around this time include unfavourable descriptions of Copenhagen's élite, who were often unable, he felt, to differentiate between exuberant behaviour and misconduct.) Nielsen never disclosed whether or not he based any of the characters on any of his pretentious contemporaries.

The masked ball provided Nielsen with an ideal setting for merriment and sparkling music. The humour is based on the encounters between characters crossing social barriers and conventions. As the dignified people reveal their hypocrisies, the audience laughs nervously, some possibly catching glimpses of themselves. Beneath the surface of the work acute perceptions flow from the subtlety and humour of its gifted creators.

Nielsen's compositions were often completed on the strength of the adrenalin which welled up immediately before a première, and on this occasion the theatre had imposed a deadline for Act I of *Maskarade* to be in full score if the opera was to be considered for inclusion in the following season's plans. The pencil score was completed on 21 May 1905 and the inked score five days later. Act II was written between 1 and 27 June. Nielsen was very proud of its speed of composition, coming as it did after a period without inspiration. Work on Act III filled his summer, but the deadline of 9 October for the completed score was fast approaching. Even with his dedicated friend Henrik Knudsen copying the ink score hard on the heels of the composition, the opera was unfinished and an overture not even started. An unconvincing finale of a few chords was added in the hope that Svendsen, now approaching his retirement, would overlook the problem (either through negligence or kindness). The gamble paid off and the work was accepted for production the following season. The score was returned to Nielsen on 21 November for completion.

A change of plans at the theatre postponed the spring 1906 production of *Maskarade*. The Theatre Royal was mounting a production of Holger Drachmann's drama *Hr. Oluf han rider* ('Sir Oluf, He Rides') to celebrate the playwright's sixtieth birthday, and Nielsen had agreed to write the music. During the summer of that year he was busy composing the music and attending rehearsals for the production, and these activities precluded any relaxation over his summer vacation, even with the generous assistance of two supportive

The first page of the score of Nielsen's satirical opera *Maskarade*

friends. He took his work to the seclusion of a boarding house at Skagen, Denmark's most northerly coast. There the landlady gave him the use of a room with a piano and his loyal friends Henrik Knudsen and the Dutch composer Julius Röntgen received mailed bundles of pencilled scribblings which they turned into neat scores. The drama described the knight Sir Oluf's powerful attraction to an elf-girl, although he cannot forget his betrothed. Little Helle's Song and the Dance Song are sung by a bold maid-servant who possesses magical powers including clairvoyance, and is revealed at the end to be Sir Oluf's mother.

*Maskarade* had been rescheduled for 11 November 1906 and permission was granted for Nielsen to conduct it even though he was no longer a member of the Theatre. Preparations were well advanced by 25 September when Nielsen began to write the overture which was completed only eight days before the opening night. (In its stage

*Maskarade* receiving
its British première in
Opera North's acclaimed
1990 production

version, the overture gives way to Act I but a concert version of
the overture was prepared with its own finale for a performance the
following year by the Stockholm Philharmonic Orchestra under
the conductor Tor Aulin. This concert version quickly became a
Nielsen sampler and a favourite choice for Danish orchestras when
touring abroad.)

While composing and rehearsing *Maskarade* many tasks fell to him
in the absence of proper theatre management. This brought about
exhaustion and some disappointment in his colleagues. Only after the
opera's success did people begin to work enthusiastically. Many
rumours and negative expectations built up before the opening night
but it was widely acknowledged that Nielsen had succeeded with
the work, despite the fears that he could not adapt his style to write
music for a comic opera. The first audiences were very enthusiastic.
The reviews found fault only in Andersen's libretto and resumed the
controversy about the propriety of touching the original work of a
revered playwright. Grieg wrote to commend Nielsen for the opera.

Early in 1907 Carl Nielsen did little else but conduct *Maskarade*,
eat and sleep. His wife fell ill at this time and for nine weeks his days
were taken up by domestic chores and hospital visits. In June Marie
recovered and he took her on a recuperative holiday to Kullen,
Norway, where they went walking in the mountains. When he began
to seek creative tasks again, he wrote not music but poetry; he took
these poems sufficiently seriously to disclose to a few friends that he
was preparing them for publication.

During Nielsen's lifetime *Maskarade* was produced in Copenhagen's
Theatre Royal in 1911, 1918, 1922–25, and the fiftieth performance
was given on 25 November 1925. The first production of the complete
opera outside Denmark took place in Gothenberg on 15 December
1930; outside Denmark it has been unjustifiably neglected and was not
performed in the United States until 1972. In the summer of 1990 it
received its British professional première to favourable popular and
critical acclaim. A sparkling production of the opera shows it to be
one of the most transparent windows to Nielsen's soul; and only when
it is stale will *Maskarade* seem to lack substance in comparison
with the symphonies. To this day it is unchallenged as *the* Danish
national opera.

*6*

Nielsen the conductor, portrayed in an oil painting by Viggo Johansen (1906). It was widely agreed that no one could rival Nielsen's ability to conduct his own symphonies.

*The plain and simple has become mysterious because the world of art as a whole has been so full of unrest, din, excitement, and delirium for so long ... The drunkard finds it hard to be content with spring water, the harlot with morning prayers, the gambler with playing forfeits. Yet they were all unspoilt at birth. But they have forgotten it, and it is hard to get back to the simple and primitive.*

Carl Nielsen, *Living Music*, 1925

# Confrontations and Crises 1907-14

The String Quartet in F major (No. 4) was Nielsen's last and most distinguished contribution to the genre. Composed between February and July 1906, it shares the joyful spirit of *Maskarade*, and is a brilliant and witty conversation between four independent voices. In August 1906 he wrote to his friend Knudsen from his friends' estate at Fuglsang, saying: 'Today we played my new quartet and it sounds as I expected. I am starting to know the true nature of string instruments. It is indeed peculiar that one can court and cajole a tender being such as a string quartet for many years before she surrenders. Only now do I consider myself to have reached some sort of accord with its chaste, fugitive character.'

Simpson has described the F major quartet as 'in every way ... the most perfect and original of all four'. But it seems less profound than its predecessor, the E flat, possessing particularly in its final two movements much of the comic mood and delicacy of *Maskarade*. It was entitled *Piacevolezza* after the first movement, 'Allegro piacevole ed indolente' (agreeably and lazily). When published in 1923 by Peters in Leipzig, this title was discarded, and the work dedicated to the Copenhagen String Quartet.

Following its première, on 30 November 1907, these musicians did much to make the work well-known, a courageous undertaking indeed, for at the time most people agreed with Kjerulf's opinion published in *Politiken* on 1 December 1907: 'If what those four gentlemen sat there playing last night in all earnestness is to be considered beautiful and good music ... then sciatica is a musical treat – for it, too, is very disagreeable.'

Nielsen felt that the quartet's ending was unsatisfactory, that it sounded as if all interest in the piece had been lost. He told a pupil, Ludvig Dolleris, that the ending had been an impulse, suggested by the image of an old man sitting in front of his house with pipe in hand. Sources reveal that Nielsen later decided to write a different ending, but none has yet been found.

After this work Nielsen abandoned the genre – to the regret of many admirers then and now. Perhaps he did so because he believed that he had taken the string quartet to the highest point he could achieve. It was his nature to move on to new challenges rather than consolidate on compositions with which he was satisfied.

'In order to win acclaim,' Nielsen had written to Knudsen in 1904, quoting Mozart, 'one must write things so simple that any fiacre driver could sing them, but also things so complex and profound that they are incomprehensible to the ordinary man; for that reason they will give pleasure to you.' These words are a key to understanding why Nielsen's œuvre contained both high-brow and more popular music. His musical 'high art' was becoming impressively complex – with the notable exception of *Maskarade* – yet his writing of songs also cost him effort. He often found the simplest melody the hardest to write. But he responded quickly to a challenge from Holger Drachmann early in 1906 to compose a song for a revue in the Tivoli gardens. By the end of their lunch together Nielsen claimed that the tune for the song was in his head. The revue in question has long since been forgotten, but *Du danske Mand* ('The Song of the Fatherland') is an enduring patriotic song first published in June 1906 and still selling well.

In 1907 he received the standard fee of 50 DKr for another song which was to earn substantial sums of money for his publishers. This song, *Jens Vejmand* ('Jens the Road-mender'), was truly Nielsen's 'greatest hit'. First recorded around 1909 by Vilhelm Herold on cylinder, by 1910 it had been arranged as a polka and for a jazz band and since then has been performed and released in every possible format. Pop versions have achieved recent chart successes in Denmark, and it has even been the subject of a documentary film. *Jens Vejmand* was based on a so-called socialist–realist text by the Danish poet Jeppe Aakjær, which in 1910 was to inspire an oil painting by Hans Smidth (1839–1917). Aakjær's poem tells of the miserable plight of an old man who works in all weathers to break down stones for roads. On a wet day the hammer slips from his hands and he loses his life; all that stands to mark his grave is a miserable board with peeling paint. Nielsen's song inspired by this text was first performed professionally by Johanne Krarup-Hansen, accompanied by Henrik Knudsen, and its directness of musical style perfectly captured the worker's plight.

*Following page, Jens Vejmand by Hans Smidth (1910). Jeppe Aakjær's poem of the impoverished road-mender had inspired Nielsen's song of the same name, one of the most popular he composed.*

The tune is so catchy that it is hard to explain why it is not known outside Denmark, where it is extremely popular.

Neither Nielsen nor his wife was wealthy although by this point their artistic careers and prospects were secure. To enable Marie to be near her studio, the family had moved in 1906 to Ny Toldbogade, near St. Anne Plads. This was a modern flat with plumbing and electricity, conveniently located for an increasing stream of visiting artists and friends. Marie was invited to exhibit in Berlin at this time and she also succeeded in selling a number of bronzes to the Dresden Museum. On 26 January that year King Christian IX had died, and a competition was announced for the commission to create a memorial monument. The competition committee advised Marie against entering on account of her gender. Nothing daunted, however, she went ahead and won the commission – one of the happiest moments of her life – but from the beginning this task meant trouble for her long-suffering family. By 1908 she needed a new home with a larger studio and the family moved again, to Vodroffsvej 53, an old villa which had belonged to a painter. Marie built a bridge to the well-lit

Carl and Anne Marie photographed in 1908 in their garden at Vodroffsvej, with the family dog Jutte

attic studio (the ceiling of which was twenty feet from the floor) which could accommodate a life-sized equestrian monument and scaffolding. The door of Nielsen's music room, which overlooked the street, was lined with felt so that he could work without disturbance. His household had never been busier. Before the move to the villa, however, he had found some time to spend some of his earnings from *Maskarade* on a hill-walking holiday in Switzerland with Vilhelm Andersen and Julius Lehman (a friend from the theatre).

In 1908 there emerged another of Nielsen's influential essays – 'Words, Music, and Programme Music' – in which the composer rejected the Symbolists' agenda of mixing the arts, demolishing in a few sentences a number of widely held conceptions, one being that music has its origin in language. He considered the independence and purity of absolute music to be paramount; it affected the composing method. 'Music neither can nor will bind itself to concrete ideas.' He felt that this might explain the riddle of why music, more than any other art, relentlessly revealed its source – the composer.

*Saga-drøm* ('Saga Dream'), however, was not absolute music, in so far as it was inspired by one of the Icelandic sagas. It was the first of Nielsen's three tone poems, completed on 1 April 1908 and given its first performance six days later. Its source was part of the Icelandic legend of *Njal's Saga*, in which Gunnar of Hlidarend rides over Tjors River, becomes weary and falls asleep, whereupon he dreams that he is being pursued by wolves – the dream proves to be prophetic. *Saga-drøm* is a colourful and popular piece that lasts only ten minutes; it begins in dream-like shadow, into which a haunting theme intrudes; despite a more active middle section the overall mood is Nordic, with a soothing chorale, and spellbinding stillness. The powerful imagery of *Njal's Saga* had also inspired what is widely considered to be Marie's greatest work before her marriage – her model of Egill Skallagrimsson bearing his son's corpse on an Icelandic mare moving forward into a strong wind.

With Johan Svendsen's retirement that year Nielsen finally achieved his aim – of being appointed conductor of the Royal Orchestra from 1 August 1908, initially on an equal footing with Svendsen's former assistant, Frederik Rung. Here was a clash of opposites: Rung was thorough and workmanlike; Nielsen on the other hand could inspire the orchestra to great heights when conducting works he liked but would lose interest on other occasions. He had begun this position with high hopes but found conditions very harrowing. His performance of Wagner's *Die Meistersinger* was attacked by his opponents, who would not forget the occasion of Ambroise Thomas's opera *Mignon*, when Rung had to take over from Nielsen in the middle of the performance: Nielsen's mind had drifted, he lost the place and his nerve. Declaring himself 'persecuted as an artist and servant of the public, and in all respects trampled upon as a nonentity from all sides', full of gloom, he cancelled a concert of his own music in Berlin, compensation for which cost him several thousand marks. Even worse, Nielsen's children had to listen to gossip about their incapable father at school. 'In brief: press attacks, misunderstandings, lies and evil, pettiness and foolishness from all those who think that they have the right to judge art in Denmark. But I do not allow myself to be affected by it and still stand firmly upon my own two feet.'

For five years Nielsen struggled against opposition, intrigues and attempts to subordinate his position in the Theatre Royal. His interest at this time was increasingly focused on dramatic rather than symphonic music, but difficulties for him at the theatre frustrated any ambitions he had to write operas. Thus Nielsen never did establish a new tradition of Scandinavian opera. In the event his greatest music is symphonic, and his dramatic music was composed mostly for ephemeral stage works – plays which are long forgotten although individual songs and instrumental pieces from them have survived.

On 8 February 1908, Copenhagen's Folk Theatre opened with L. C. Nielsen's play *Willemoes.* Its subject was the young Danish naval hero, Peter Willemoes, a cousin of N. F. S. Grundtvig (founder of the Danish Folk High School Movement). The hero had gone down with his ship in 1808 on a naval engagement with the English. Sadly, the play sank without such foreign intervention, but Carl Nielsen's stirring song, *Havet omkring Danmark* ('The Sea Around Denmark'), survived as an alternative national anthem. *Tove,* a play by the poet Ludvig Holstein, has also been consigned to oblivion, but four songs from it by Nielsen were published: one of them, *Vi sletternes sønner* ('We Sons of the Plains'), captured the eerie half-light of the Danish dusk with the effect of 'the dreams we sons of the plains are possessed … and know not until they shatter.' In 1909 Nielsen wrote two songs for Jeppe Aakjær's play *Ulvens søn* ('The Wolf's Son'): *Kommer i snart, i husmænd* ('Are You Coming Soon, Smallholders?') is a call for action, urging the hard-pressed tenants to take things into their own hands; *Gamle Anders Røgters Sang* ('Old Anders the Cowherd's Song') laments that life depends so much on circumstances: we can rarely rise above them because 'we trample over one another in the mire.' Nielsen's setting of Aakjær's *Som dybest brønd* ('Like the Deepest Well'), written during World War I, became very popular through its powerful depiction of the Danish predicament. 'You tiny country, hiding snugly in your cradle while the world around you is ablaze.' On 4 June 1910 in the open-air theatre at Ulvedalene, north of Copenhagen, *Hagbarth og Signe* by Adam Oehlenschlæger was first produced, for which Nielsen wrote a dance and *My Helmet Gleams and Heavy is to Bear* (Halloge's Song). The play concerns Hagbarth, who, having killed his beloved Signe's brother in a duel, sits imprisoned awaiting execution. (Halloge is the bard who expresses the hero's grief.)

Nielsen seems to have been content in these years although long-term domestic and career problems must have been in their early stages. From 1908 Marie became obsessed with the monument to Christian IX and the family was disrupted by her continued long absences abroad, long hours of work at home and vast financial disbursements. From the moment of winning the commission she fought hard for what she wanted and persuaded the committee to provide the funds she needed. For most of 1909 she stayed at the German village of Celle purely to study the breed of horses favoured by Christian IX for his statue. Nielsen visited her there, leaving his work behind, and also went to see his younger daughter Søs in London, where she was at boarding school. Søs accompanied her father to the newly established Henry Wood Promenade Concerts. And while in London Nielsen made arrangements for Marie to have an exhibition there although nothing was to come of it.

Nielsen could depend on a small circle of friends and admirers for support, but, as is clear from the correspondence between Celle and Copenhagen, he keenly missed the advice and encouragement of his wife. He had become so downcast in 1910 that the housekeeper, Maren, purchased a savings bond with her meagre wages which she presented to her master 'so that you need not worry and struggle with people'. But Nielsen was not inclined to solitude and his friendship with the Neergaard family introduced him to artistic circles and some

Anne Marie in her studio at
Celle in Germany, where she
stayed in 1909 to prepare
the equestrian monument to
King Christian IX

stimulating conversation. They gathered over successive summers at the Neergaard's estate of Fuglsang on Lolland, an island south of Jylland. The estate owner, Rolf Viggo Neergaard, was married to J. P. E. Hartmann's granddaughter, Bodil. Her brother was the painter Oluf Hartmann who died in January 1910 aged only thirty, and in whose memory Nielsen wrote *Ved en ung kunstners baare* ('At the Bier of a Young Artist'). Played at Hartmann's funeral, it is an evocative piece with a mood of lingering sadness ('Andante Lamentoso'). Only five minutes long, it was initially scored for string quintet and subsequently transcribed for string orchestra.

During the time he was hard at work in Copenhagen, Nielsen could rely on letters from Bodil Neergaard, and each Christmas his family received gifts from her. In 1913, having received the present of a deer, he wrote a moving letter of thanks: 'When I saw the legs of the

Rolf Viggo and Bodil Neergaard pictured in front of their home at Fuglsang. Their hospitality over many summers from 1905 provided Nielsen with a welcome retreat from Copenhagen.

deer sticking out, I saw you, dear Bodil, Viggo, Skejten, Aunt Bolette, Omand's pictures, the Christmas tree, Nina, Tony, Lehmann, the swans, the bat, the Hole, the moon, Petersen, the garden, Marie Neergaard, the bicycles, Koaléen, Hansens the gardener all together in a bewildering daze ... I shouldn't be surprised if these intense, unreasonable and sudden longings herald something to come in the near future. I believe so. In a few years an aeroplane will be a common sight, so that we, who belong together in all that is vital and most important, may be together when we like.' The countryside, and thinking about the countryside, was an essential retreat from the pressures of Copenhagen. A letter to Bodil of February 1916 explains some of his strong feelings towards Fuglsang:

*When both my parents were still alive and I was a child on Fyn, it always happened that when the world went against me and I was desperate and bored with everything, then this thought would come, together with a strong feeling of longing: now I shall go home; now that I cannot go on any longer, I shall go home ... Something of this feeling has passed over to Fuglsang. It is as though a good friend were standing behind me, something secure that continues to be there and is a comfort.*

Nielsen and his family spent many happy summers at Fuglsang. During the days he enjoyed horse-riding, sailing, and bathing in the sea. Fine dinners were enjoyed, followed by chamber music (sometimes Nielsen's recent compositions) performed by professional musicians who stayed there each summer. Bodil Neergaard herself sang on occasion, becoming, as Søs put it, 'quite another person; gone was the affable smile of the hostess, a dream-like intensity possessed her.'

In the seclusion of the summer house at Fuglsang Nielsen often worked late into the evening. One dark August night he was so late that everyone in the music room worried about where he was. Eventually he came up the path towards the house and knocked on a window. He had emerged from the grounds looking quite bewildered. In some distress, he told his assembled and concerned friends that he had been in the woods when darkness fell, had lost his bearings and walked aimlessly, guided only by the trees whose branches were striking his eyes and cracking under his steps. Seized by panic he had

Chamber music in Fulgsang:
'Today we played my string
quartet and it sounds as I
expected.' Nielsen's String
Quartet in F Major was first
performed in the music room
at Fuglsang in 1906.
Nielsen is performing the
quartet with (from left to
right) the Dutch composers
Gerard von Brucken-Fock
and Julius Röntgen, and
Röntgen's son Engelbert.

fallen on all fours, sweating profusely, his heart hammering, and had finally found his way back to the house.

It was at Fuglsang that Nielsen first met the Dutch composer Julius Röntgen. He was, alongside Busoni, one of the first European composers to promote Nielsen's music beyond Denmark, and with the pianist Henrik Knudsen, he was at this time one of the composer's most willing helpers; his support would be lifelong. Nielsen suffered pangs of conscience because he never refused help, yet felt that Knudsen took on far too much on his behalf. Röntgen was also reassured by Nielsen of his gratitude and friendship. Two years previously Nielsen had confided to him: 'We really only write for the good musicians, and have our reward in that we are understood and appreciated by them. Therefore, dear friend, I am so thankful for your friendship ...'

Returning from Fuglsang to the city was torture. In the two seasons from 1910 to 1912, Nielsen had to endure, with increasing resentment

'I am so thankful for your friendship': Nielsen to the Dutch composer Julius Röntgen (right)

'Ah God! Henrik, one day we'll have some peace and quiet': Nielsen to the pianist Henrik Knudsen, one of his closest collaborators

and frustration, the restrictive conditions of his employment as conductor at the Copenhagen Theatre. He must have experienced long periods of despair and isolation because of the campaign of persecution which is only hinted at in his letters from this period. He became further exasperated when in the autumn of 1911 Marie returned to Celle. On 22 September he wrote to her from Copenhagen:

*Hello! Is there anyone there? ... Please be so good as to tell us something about yourself. Have you begun modelling? How are things going with you, my dear? You must not worry about us. Søs is so busy, and Hans Børge is so regular with his work, which is marvellous. Irmelin is really the only one who seems to have lost her way. She behaves so strangely and seems so undecided, especially as she has just had a cold. I am working on my concerto, slowly but with real certainty. The task is most difficult and therefore interesting ... Things are peaceful and well at the theatre now. I am satisfied with the conditions and everyone is friendly towards me.*

In 1911 under these stable but not always happy conditions, which were soon to collapse along with Europe's peace, Nielsen completed his Violin Concerto and Third Symphony, the two works which first established him as a major European composer. The concerto for the violin, one of his cherished musical ambitions, had been begun that summer. On the invitation of the family's dear friends, the two sisters Toni Hagerup and Nina (widow of the Norwegian composer Edvard Grieg), Nielsen and his friend Julius Lehmann visited their famous home, Troldhaugen, near Bergen in Norway. In Grieg's hut, nicknamed 'Komposten', Nielsen had set to work on the concerto.

*You can't imagine how delightful it is up here in Norway, especially in the evenings, when the mountain tops stand out against the clear heavens. We are right down by the water and can row around the romantic little islands and islets, going for quite a long time all alone and fancy that we are the only people in the world. You simply cannot guess how sweet they are, these two small people. Nina is completely like a hostess and housewife, everything is in order ...*

In July Nielsen returned to Copenhagen, then continued work on the concerto at Damgaard, another of his retreats, near Kolding in

Jylland. But the work was put aside when theatre rehearsals began on 1 September, and was not completed until mid December. The break in the work's composition gave rise to the comment – first raised by the Hungarian composer Ernő Dohnányi – that it is divided into two discernible styles. Nielsen had a soloist with an international reputation in mind: his friend Peder Møller, who the previous year had returned to Denmark from Paris to lead the Royal Orchestra. And on 28 February 1912 when the work was given its first performance in Copenhagen's Odd Fellow Hall, it was played by Møller with the Royal Orchestra, conducted by the composer. Møller also took the concerto to Stockholm, Gothenburg, Oslo, Berlin and Paris.

At the same time a promising twenty-year-old Hungarian violinist, Emil Telmányi, had arrived in Copenhagen in search of an audience. He met Carl Nielsen immediately after the composer had completed his concerto, but it had been written for Møller. It was only later that Telmányi was to play an important role in Nielsen's life.

Nielsen's classical heritage is evident in the Violin Concerto. The structure was traditional (although there are only two movements,

The violinist Peder Møller, *left*, gave the first performance of Nielsen's Violin Concerto in 1912. Subsequently the Hungarian violinist Emil Telmányi, *right*, was to be an enthusiastic champion of the concerto and of Nielsen's work in general.

they are separated by an intermezzo, a substitute for the conventional slow movement), and harmonically and rhythmically Nielsen clung again to a Classical restraint. The concerto introduced elements that became mainstays of his concerto-writing – antiphonal writing between soloist and orchestra, sequential passages and frequent cadenzas. Genial and relaxed as it is, the concerto has never been considered one of Nielsen's best works – it would be outclassed by the later concertos for flute and clarinet – but the relative lack of appreciation of the work must in part be due to the phenomenal success of Nielsen's Third Symphony, *Sinfonia espansiva*, which had its première at the same time.

The first two movements of *Sinfonia espansiva* had been written at Damgaard. The main theme for its third movement, which he once referred to as the symphony's heartbeat, came to him on a tram-car and was sketched on the cuff of his shirt. He worked on the Finale over the winter of 1910–11, completing the symphony on 30 April 1911. His friend, Thorvald Nielsen, recalled his memories as an orchestral violinist rehearsing the Third Symphony a few days before its première. 'The orchestra had gathered, Nielsen sat down, gave the signal – and shot after shot thundered from the roaring orchestra with ever increasing rapidity as if to force out the theme – then it came. At this moment Nielsen turned pale – and sat up in his chair. We played the whole movement through without stopping. After the terrific orchestral storm and under the impression of the grandiose music, we all felt quite out of breath. Everybody realized that we had been present at a historic moment. And the concert at the Odd Fellow Hall turned out to be a great triumph for Nielsen.'

Under the composer's baton *Sinfonia espansiva* was his greatest success to date. Performances were immediately requested abroad and it seemed that Nielsen had not only found his voice but was achieving recognition as a leading composer. His critics, if not silenced, now had to attack a composer whose reputation at home and abroad was secure.

Perhaps because Nielsen felt that he had now made good in Copenhagen despite his past trials and tribulations, this symphony is Nielsen's most optimistic and perhaps therefore his most charac-teristic. It radiates an intense and joyous exuberance, and is expansive both in gesture and thematic growth. In spite of the work's strong

Nielsen at the piano composing the Third Symphony, the work that was to secure his international reputation

Classical feel, largely communicated by expansive themes over busy rhythmic activity, ever increasing dissonance verges on polytonality. Some moments are exquisite, such as towards the end of the second movement when soprano and baritone soloists wordlessly intone the vowel 'a'. Nielsen here was aiming at 'a sort of phlegmatically paradisal mood'.

The symphony was described as 'the new dominant element in twentieth-century music ... rhythm now makes its entry into the Danish symphony.' To the Norwegian newspaper, *Verdens Gang*, the composer declared his aims: 'I am – or better – I was often a bone of contention ... because I wanted to protest against the typical Danish soft smoothing over. I want stronger rhythms and more advanced harmony.' Nielsen's Third Symphony might be said to have served notice on Danish musicians on the new direction of music – there was no longer to be polite instrumentation and agreeable harmonies, but rather something stirring and active. When the music of the symphony relaxes in serene bliss or pastoral tranquillity, it is only recuperating in order to gain new strength. Nielsen was to provide a programme note for a performance in Copenhagen on 14 January 1927 by the newly-founded Danish Radio Symphony Orchestra, talking of the strong tension (espansiva) of the first movement which is completely eradicated in the second movement by idyllic calm. For an even later performance in Stockholm in 1931, he wrote: 'The third movement is something that cannot really be characterized in that both good and evil make themselves felt without a real character. The Finale, on the other hand, is straightforward: a hymn to work and the healthy enjoyment of daily life. *Not* a pathetic celebration of life but a sort of general joy in being able to participate in the business of everyday living and to see activity and skill unfold all around us.' Man quite literally is at the centre of Nielsen's art, yet without any 'programme'; this is pure and absolute music.

After the première in the Odd Fellow Hall, a concert arranged by Nielsen himself, he was immediately asked to conduct *Sinfonia espansiva* at the Theatre Royal. He gave three performances there in May, having conducted it in Holland on 28 April 1912 thanks to arrangements made by Röntgen. In January the following year, when Nielsen conducted the work in Stuttgart, a critic described it as 'a mighty animating call from the north'; Nielsen reckoned that day to be the greatest day of his life. In December 1913 his family gathered in Berlin to attend a well-rehearsed performance of the symphony conducted by Siegmund von Hausegger. Nielsen was pleased with the performance, but the critics were not unanimous in high praise. Warsaw, Hamburg, Göteborg and Oslo gave the work better receptions.

During the summer of 1912 Nielsen had an encounter which he later described as 'the most remarkable, indeed the greatest in my life'. He was weeding his garden when he looked up and saw a man who asked in broken Danish if he was speaking to Carl Nielsen. If so, perhaps he might be able to recognize the inquirer. At that moment Nielsen, in amazement, identified his brother, Peter, who had been in Australia and who had not seen his brother Carl in thirty-four years. They telegraphed the news of the reunion to their five brothers and sisters who had settled in Chicago. Sophus came in response. The three brothers then travelled to their native Fyn and spent several days reliving memories, playing their childrens' games, and talking about their present lives.

In 1913 the German music publishers C. F. Kahnt paid Nielsen 5,000 DM for the symphony, more than six times the sum he could expect from his Danish publishers. But it was a short-lived association, partly due to the outbreak of war but there is also some evidence that Nielsen suspected Kahnt of certain irregularities. While Marie was in Celle she was summoned to Dresden where Irmelin, a student at the Jacques Dalcroze school of dancing, had been taken ill. Being so close to Leipzig Marie took the opportunity of visiting the Kahnt premises, pretending to be a singer making enquiries about the Danish symphony, in order to expose the publishers' lack of enthusiasm in handling the work. Hausegger also made a claim that the publishers had offered to hire the score to an orchestra, thereby contravening the agreed terms which specified outright sale of the first twenty copies.

After two of the most enthusiastic receptions of the Third Symphony, in Helsinki and Stockholm in November 1913, Nielsen protested to the Neergaards that the whole thing seemed so un-deserved, because his works had not got one hundredth part of what he wanted and had aimed for. 'When I have noticed the warm applause from the orchestra and public, I have often felt so very embarrassed and have wanted to say, "Ah, but you should know how far all this is from my true desire. Thanks for your good intentions but now I must take greater pains in future and reach a higher plane."'

During the 1912–13 season Nielsen worked excessively, taking on all conducting duties while also composing his ground-breaking Sonata No. 2 for Violin and Piano, which was completed on 13 September 1912. For its première on 7 April 1913 at the Odd Fellow Hall, Peder Møller was indisposed and Axel Gade (son of Niels Gade) stepped in at short notice to replace him, accompanied by Henrik Knudsen.

While the work boasted a typical Nielsen structural clarity, its tonal scheme was now totally liberated and a traditional form absent; the Brahms of the first violin and piano sonata of sixteen years earlier had been left behind, superseded by a more avant-garde music that anticipated Béla Bartók in its modernism. The fast change of pace, the swift progress through keys, the sudden rhythmic jolts – all combined to shock its first listeners. The composer and violinist Fini Henriques, one of Nielsen's admirers, lost his patience after hearing the sonata, and confronted Nielsen: 'Now look here, Carl, this is a damned affectation.' He was especially critical of the hammering B flat towards the end of the Finale but Nielsen was adamant that it should be retained: without that passage, he said, the ending of the sonata would collapse like a pack of cards.

The sonata made slow progress after its initial rebuff by audience and critics alike but it was eventually published by Hansen in 1919 (as No. 2; the first published Sonata was, incidentally, not numbered because of an early unpublished work). In this printed edition Nielsen's initial token reference to the key of G minor was dropped in recognition of the work's free tonality. In 1914 Nielsen took some pride in its performance in Amsterdam by Telmányi and the celebrated Austrian pianist Artur Schnabel, who had heard the work on a visit to Copenhagen. The printed edition of 1919 incorporated some suggestions made by Schnabel, supposedly made at enhancing the timbre, but in later performances with Telmányi, Nielsen reverted to his original intentions. Telmányi subsequently edited it in this form, which is now generally preferred and considered authentic.

An avant-garde work was all his critics needed to undermine the success generated by the Third Symphony. In August 1913 Marie returned from Germany to unveil her statue of Queen Dagmar and she and her husband agreed that they would both make better progress in Germany. But Carl hesitated in joining her and then, with the death on 22 January 1914 of Frederik Rung, fate intervened. Nielsen entertained hopes that he would finally take up the conducting position he had in effect already fulfilled. The management was, however, divided and indecisive. At first they appointed Georg Høeberg as second Kapellmeister under Nielsen. But they considered further, and Høeberg, who had been received with excessive praise, was elevated to the rank of Kapellmeister alongside Nielsen. The two conductors were expected to share authority and responsibility. Nielsen wrote from Göteborg to the theatre director rejecting this arrangement, well aware that by doing so he was risking his economic security and connection to the theatre. 'This is the third piece of paper I have begun ... My thoughts circle round and round. From my earliest youth I have fought, worked, erred, triumphed, been cast down, risen up again, but have all the same kept to a certain straight line in my endeavours ... I cannot easily break off and begin, so to speak, all over again ...' After discussing what he had endured in the past as a subordinate to the First Kapellmeister, Nielsen ended by stating that he did not think the proposed arrangement of unspecified responsibilities was feasible.

As the management failed to keep its promises to Nielsen, the composer left the theatre at the end of May 1914. Having first left the Royal Orchestra after sixteen years' service as a violinist, and then being forced to resign again after a further six years conducting, he was in despair. To the leader of the orchestra, Anton Svendsen, he wrote: 'I don't believe that I am by nature of a sentimental disposition, but when I left you today I had a lump in my throat. I have not felt so strongly moved for many years, and only thus can I understand myself: that your glance and your handshake radiated something of the warmth which, without knowing it and wanting or daring to ask for, I have for so long a time needed so terribly, more terribly than anyone suspects.'

War in Europe was looming and Nielsen's frequently postponed hopes of working in Germany if all went wrong at home were dashed. The scale of bloodshed soon became apparent, and every day Nielsen went to the town square to read frightful figures of incomprehensible slaughter. To the Scandinavians not directly involved in the conflict the humanitarian issues, devoid of nationalistic bias, appeared sharper. Nielsen despaired but saw the necessity of a cyclical upturn. To Beckman he wrote:

> ... it's as if the whole world is disintegrating. What will become of it? It's bad enough that the material world is being destroyed and that men murder each other but that is nothing compared to the horror of European men of intellect and spirit losing their reason and becoming mad! National feeling, that until now was distinguished as something lofty and beautiful, has become a spiritual syphilis that has eaten away their brains, and it grins hideously through empty eye-sockets with dreadful hatred. What sort of a germ is it that is destroying the finest minds of the warring nations? It is so excessive and meaningless; life seems to be worth nothing ... Maybe it will pass over like so much evil in the world. But I do wish for one thing: that this war may not end until the whole of the civilized world lies in ruins! Now we must go to the bitter end! Now we must really be prepared. This must never happen again and so it must be done with a vengeance.

The seven years that had led up to World War I had epitomized Nielsen's search for inner peace. He had become used to the struggle that was necessary for his music to be accepted. Opportunities to take his work to more broad-minded ears abroad were not acted upon, and then with the outbreak of war, became impossible. Nielsen was left as the proverbial big fish in a small pond.

# 7

## Songs and a 'War Symphony' 1914–16

Nielsen with his daughter
Irmelin, who choreographed
the dance scenes for the
open-air theatre production
of *Elverskud*

*The claims of life are stronger than the most
sublime art; and even were we to agree that we
had achieved the best and most beautiful it is
possible to achieve, we should be impelled in
the end, thirsting as we do for life and experience than for perfection, to cry out, 'Give us
something else; give us something new; for
Heaven's sake give us something bad, so long as
we feel we are alive and active and not just
passive admirers of tradition!'*

Carl Nielsen, *Living Music*, 1925

# Songs and a 'War Symphony' 1914–16

Very few of Nielsen's friends seem to have known that he wanted to live abroad for reasons other than his limited career success in Denmark until, towards the end of 1914, his wife's application for an official legal separation became public knowledge. The *de facto* separation chosen by his wife in pursuit of her career was no extenuating plea at law – legally it was Carl Nielsen who was the guilty party on the ground of his adulterous liaison. The ensuing separation in 1915 rendered him homeless but still responsible for the upkeep of his family.

Under the terms of his daughters' bequest of documents that form the core of the Carl Nielsen Archive (housed in Copenhagen's Royal Library), the literary documents cannot yet be accessed by researchers. In addition to these, it is possible that illuminating rather than merely prurient documents exist which are not even listed in the Archive. The musical manuscripts, on the other hand, have been fully and conscientiously catalogued.

Nielsen's elder daughter, Irmelin, handed his letters and diaries to the leading authority on Nielsen, Torben Schousboe, and he was allowed to study them before handing them over in the mid 1970s to the national collection in Copenhagen's Royal Library. Schousboe's 1983 edition of the diaries and correspondence between the couple is heavily edited – particularly when covering the years from 1915 when the couple separated. Otherwise the edition is brilliant and authoritative. Irmelin requested that the documents remain under an embargo for twenty-five years after Schousboe's edition. This excessive secrecy goes far towards explaining the lack of Nielsen biographies to date – only fairly narrow perspectives have been published, in Danish, and they have not been reprinted.

The essence of Nielsen's errant behaviour is well known in Denmark yet librarians and academics, claiming moral and political correctness, tend to ignore it. Biographers have reacted, it would seem, according to personal bias. While one stressed his 'weakness of character with women, numerous liaisons and illegitimate children', others excused his behaviour by pointing to his often extreme solitude and his need for company while Anne Marie worked away from home for long periods. (In 1912 Carl did have an affair with a member of Copenhagen's Theatre Royal, and a daughter was born, named Rachel Siegman. Placed with foster parents, she stayed in touch with her father, and like the boy born out of wedlock to Nielsen, she studied at the Copenhagen Conservatoire and is known to have composed some music.)

Carl Nielsen was by 1915 a celebrated man of considerable wit, charm and magnetism. In his quiet, unassuming way his presence attracted attention and dominated gatherings. He could be gregarious, and was in many ways unrestrained by social convention, himself the son of a non-Christian father who never truly settled down and who only married after his first child was born.

Nielsen was able to compose music of a mood that contrasted with the events and circumstances of his own life. Often he would imagine nature scenes when feeling oppressed by his life in the city. Despite burgeoning marital troubles he managed to compose a piece of light

The music room at Frederiksholm Kanal 28a, Copenhagen, where Nielsen lived from 1915 until his death in 1931. The room was reconstructed in 1988 at the Carl Nielsen Museum in Odense.

music, *Serenata in Vano* ('A Serenade in Vain'). The bassist, Anton Hegner, a friend of Nielsen's, was touring Jylland with some members of the Royal Danish Orchestra and needed a small piece to fill out the programme. Nielsen had the idea of sending the players on an errand of romance – to serenade someone's lady-love in the country. The piece, finished on 13 May 1914 and scored for clarinet, bassoon, horn, cello and double bass, was described by its composer as being 'a humorous trifle. First the gentlemen play in a somewhat chivalrous and showy manner to lure the fair one out on to the balcony, but she does not appear. Then they play in a slightly languorous strain (*poco adagio*), but that has no effect either. Since they have played in vain (*in vano*), they don't care and give up, shuffling home to the strains of a little march, which they play for their own amusement.'

Wilhelm Stenhammar (1871-1927), Swedish composer, pianist and conductor. As Director of the Göteborg Symphony Orchestra he often invited Nielsen to Sweden as a guest conductor.

By 1914, although he was beginning to enjoy considerable success as a composer, Nielsen was not to be funded in Denmark. Unable to move to Germany, he contacted his friend Wilhelm Stenhammar, Sweden's leading composer and conductor, requesting regular employment, and this led to guest and term appointments over several seasons. Earlier that year he had conducted the Göteborg Symphony Orchestra playing *Saga-drøm* and the Violin Concerto (with Møller as soloist). Quite unlike the strife and jealousies Nielsen had experienced in Copenhagen, he enjoyed in Göteborg the respect a town never offers its own sons, and especially the friendship and patronage of the merchant banker Herman Mannheimer and his family. In fact, Nielsen forged such a rapport with the Swedish musicians that he told some friends that he respected Stenhammar for not feeling threatened.

Nielsen's creative powers from about 1906 had followed two parallel but complementary paths into both 'art' music and more popular music, as is evident from his continued enthusiasm for song-writing. From 1914 the two strands were even more apparent: he sustained two separate composing careers in addition to his conducting and teaching appointments.

At this time Nielsen seems to have been torn by a need for peace and security, and accepting a reality that did not offer such comfort. And long periods of absence from Denmark were intensifying Nielsen's patriotic feelings. 'Folk song lies close to my heart in such a way that when I write a certain melody, it is as if it were not I that composed it, but friends, kinsmen and the folk of the country who

The concert hall in Göteborg. In this city Nieslen found the appreciative audience which he could not always rely upon in his own country.

wished it so ...' Whether, or when, Nielsen would have started to write folk songs on his own initiative is open to question, but the Danish organist and church composer Thomas Laub had chosen exactly the right moment to approach Nielsen with his plan to re-enliven Danish song. Nielsen had already received a request from a priest around 1911 to write melodies to hymns by Bishop N. F. S. Grundtvig, founder of the Danish Folk High School Movement for adult education, but only a handful of melodies had come of this. Nothing at all had emerged from a similar, much earlier suggestion made by the minister of the independent church at Aagaard near Kolding.

From 1912 he had started to write some modern tunes for Danish nineteenth-century hymns. He had also been asked by Johan Borup, a leader of one of the Folk High Schools, to contribute to a Danish Song Book. Nielsen produced twenty songs. Now, with the encouragement of Thomas Laub – a friend but open protestor against Nielsen's dissonant expression of life's disagreeable forces – Nielsen began to write songs for schools, amateur and trained choirs and singers. Most of these both renewed the nation's song tradition and popularized Danish poetry from all ages (Nielsen's first songs had been set mainly to contemporary texts). The songs were powerful in their simplicity and directness of utterance – and yet, at the same time

Nielsen's more esoteric music was soaring above contemporary critical acceptance. The songs' melodies were simple and catchy compared with the more technically demanding songs that Nielsen intended for professional and stage performance. Unlike Bartók's and Kodály's conservation of traditional Hungarian folk song, Nielsen and Laub aimed instead to create a new body of popular song which would stand the test of time.

Nielsen had first met Laub in 1891 when Laub succeeded Niels W. Gade as organist at the Holmens Church in Copenhagen. Protest over his appointment, and his modern style of composition, made him the focal point of a debate which argued that the style of Danish popular and church songs was too much in the stiff tradition of the German Romantic Lied. Nielsen's sympathies were entirely with Laub and the reformers. Laub however was outspoken in his opposition to most of Nielsen's music, and as early as 1892 had reacted to the String Quintet with, 'I felt as if it was the devil, who, on a beautiful cool spring morning, was walking in his garden and busy pulling up radishes.'

Despite Laub's dislike of Nielsen's more progressive musical elements, he had admired the oratorio treatment in *Saul og David*; he could also see that Nielsen's songs from 1907 demonstrated a real ability to write tuneful melodies. Each composer was aware of the other's strength and their common ground. Laub's plan was three-point: to cleanse Danish hymns and songs of all traits of German style and Romantic ornamentation, to widen the knowledge of good Danish poems, and to create an easy style of ballad which anyone could sing. The objective of giving good people good words to sing to popular melodies was set out in a famous letter to Nielsen in 1914.

Laub was also convinced that he and Nielsen were the best people to do this: Nielsen's strength was his ability to encapsulate a mood in a simple and popular style that seemed already known to its audience; Laub's was his knowledge of church music and medieval folksong. Looking back on the fruits of their collaboration, Nielsen reflected to his friend Thorvald Aagaard: 'It's strange that there was a man like Thomas Laub on our path. He stood there fully prepared and showed us with the sharpest clarity all those things we could only see through a mist or hadn't yet arrived at, thanks to our poor development.'

Thomas Laub (1852–1927), who 'showed us with the sharpest clarity all those things we could only see through a mist or hadn't yet arrived at.' Laub's efforts to establish a simple song tradition inspired Nielsen to revitalize Danish folksong.

Their first collection of songs, *En snes danske viser* ('A Score of Danish Songs'), published by Hansen in 1915, was prefaced by Nielsen's quotation of the words of the German–Danish composer J. A. P. Schulz (1747–1800): 'In these tunes, I have taken pains to achieve the utmost clarity, indeed, I have attempted to the best of my ability to invest them with the characteristic that they appear to be already familiar. In this rests the secret of the popular song tradition.' Nielsen understood his task as being one of reviving interest in the old folk songs by publishing a collection of melodies to the best Danish poets' verse, composed in such a way that the poems themselves remained the important matter. He believed that he and Laub acted only as the musical servants who clothed the verse in the very simplest manner and in a spirit that suited the poems. The first poems were selected by Laub, who diplomatically avoided those already set to music by their esteemed predecessors – Heise, Hartmann and Gade.

On 13 April 1915 the first recital of the songs was given by the singers Emilie Ulrich, Carl Madsen and Anders Brems, with Salomon Levysohn, an event at which *Serenata in Vano* also received its première. It was a concert intended to achieve 'a certain atmosphere of cosiness'. The singers, dressed in only semi-formal clothers, sat on the platform, each rising to give a few songs, not sung in the keys of the printed edition, but transposed to suit each voice on the occasion. It was immediately apparent that these songs marked a turning-point in Danish song: the formal, ornate Romance style had been replaced by one that was more direct and authentic. The music was more accessible to ordinary people. Two years later a second collection of songs in collaboration with Laub was published, and it was first heard in Feburary 1916. These songs were enormously popular and are still favourites in Denmark today.

Nielsen, independently of Laub, published a collection of Hymns and Sacred Songs in 1919, the greater part of its poems being by Bishop Grundtvig. Old German melodies had previously been used for many of them. Nielsen felt that Danish composers needed to try to recapture Grundtvig with new Nordic melodies, as it, after all, had been the Danish nature and the Nordic way of thinking that had set Grundtvig's great mind in motion. Nielsen's melodies were the product of considerable study of post-Reformation chorales; he had tried to make the settings as clear and simple as possible, 'for one should not drink Schnapps when a glass of water would be sufficient to quench one's thirst ...'

Nielsen's preface to the manuscript, although not included in the printed edition, is worth quoting, as it describes the composer's own spiritual outlook in contrast to Laub's religious orthodoxy.

*There are some people who are always able to create a feeling of comfort and warmth around them. Usually it is neither the wittiest nor the most pronounced personalities who are endowed with these valuable characteristics: it is most often the people who least of all wish to impress or impose their opinions or taste on others. A profound feeling of benevolence tells them that it is quite pointless to attempt to reform by compulsion but that it is a question of encouraging what is good to develop by the simplest means. In this way evil will disappear of its own accord.*

*This collection of tunes is an attempt to compose from a similar basic feeling, only here my only wish is to improve the standard of hymns in this country, which, I have to admit, has often caused me to shudder. It is not always the songs in themselves but the surroundings which account for this reaction. It does not offend me to hear objectionable music issuing from the entrance to a basement passage, but in a church, in a state school, or in a good Danish home I expect and insist upon decency of speech and singing ...*

Nielsen was attracted to the spiritual, religious song, but the songs of this collection were not congregational hymns of the type to have appealed to Laub. In response to the collection, Laub criticized Nielsen's lack of religious faith, saying: 'A composer [of sacred songs] must be "Child of the House", must belong intensely ... His faith can be little and may be wrong ... but, he must be 'home', that is, must have lived within the song of the congregation, at best from childhood ...'

Nielsen – in heated discussions with his hosts at Damgaard – had also rejected such theories as Rudolf Steiner's theosophy. Although he did not have time for the more superstitious facets of Christianity, he identified the spiritual aspects of life and art as the values that are both humanistic and enduring. In 1894 he had written that 'Only deeply religious art will endure, and I take the great masters as proof of this. I don't consider that a human being must be Christian, Jew or Muslim to be able to create good art, but he must in short be filled with high and holy seriousness when he sets about his task.'

Nielsen started work on these religious songs earlier than his first cataloguers believed. The original manuscripts also reveal that many of the harmonizations were contributed by the composer and organist Paul Hellmuth – these include some of Nielsen's more popular songs, such as the chorale *Min Jesus, lad mit hjerte faa* ('My Jesus, make my heart to love Thee'), which was to become the last-movement theme in Nielsen's most performed chamber work, the Wind Quintet of 1922.

In June 1915 Marie was awarded by the government an artist's town house at a low rent. Frederiksholm Kanal 28A marked the end of her family's frequent house-moving: she would remain there for the rest of her life. Attached to a large studio, this terraced house opposite the canal had been the residence of several Danish sculptors; one of these was Vilhelm Bissen who had rejected her as a pupil many years before because she was a woman. The Nielsen family regarded this house as very grand, spacious and full of interesting features. Moving their furniture was quite an undertaking, according to Søs, her father's grand piano causing the greatest difficulty. The house was very run down. Dirty water had to be pumped out of the basement, floorboards repaired and the stairs mended. Marie persevered with the faulty stoves for a while, but was obliged to replace them. Maren made the house a centre for visitors and a comfortable home for the family. She was as ever the anchor of the household – both parents were mostly absent, Irmelin was boarding in Geneva (her school had moved there when war broke out), and Hans Børge lived in the country where he learned gardening.

Frederiksholm Kanal 28a, the Nielsens' town house from 1915. The family regarded the house as very grand, spacious and full of interesting features.

That year, 1915, the conductor of Copenhagen's Philharmonic Orchestra, Franz Neruda, died and Nielsen was unanimously elected to his post. This provided some income, continued a connection with Copenhagen's musical life, and gave him the opportunity to have music of his choice performed without having to commit too much time to the position. But otherwise, separated from his wife, Nielsen was lonely, a loneliness that deepened when his father died on 22 November. Not long after, he heard of the death of his patron and good friend, Viggo Neergaard, owner of Fuglsang. Deeply affected by both deaths, Nielsen journeyed to the Fuglsang estate to comfort Viggo's widow.

At this time he was making regular visits to Copenhagen to sit on the examination board of the Conservatoire. Here, as when playing string quartets, Nielsen never lost his playful character. About two years after his appointment to the board, at the annual festival at which new entrants were required to display their talents, Nielsen suddenly disappeared. Several new entrants had played their pieces when a stout figure in short trousers and a yellow wig climbed on to the stage with a leather case. The strangely dressed fellow took some music from his case, sat down at the piano, and played an entire movement from a Mozart sonata. The audience was in uproar, recognizing the well-known figure apparently applying to become a Conservatoire student, and howled: 'Yes, yes, he's accepted!'

Furthering his ideals of art for everyone, Nielsen also sat on the founding committee of an open-air theatre at Ulvedalene, a deer park some ten miles north of Copenhagen. He produced two works there in 1915, becoming, through the illness of both director Johannes Nielsen and producer Adam Poulsen, responsible for everything from the construction of the stage to the training of the singers. Irmelin's skills from the Dalcroze school were put to good use: she choreographed the parts for the light ballad opera, *Liden Kirsten* ('Little Kirsten'), whose music by Hartmann was set to a story by Hans Christian Andersen. The other production was that of Gade's famous choral work derived from Scandinavian folk legend, *Elverskud* ('Bewitched' – but usually rendered in English as 'Elf Shot' or 'Fairy Spell'). Gade's composition has been described as the peak of the popular Danish tradition of choral works that derived from

An advertisement for the performances of Liden Kirsten and Elverskud, both produced by Carl Nielsen

the Mendelssohn oratorio. Many excellent singers took part in the production, the technical demands of which did not tax the amateur performers, and choir and orchestra numbered 100 and 50 respectively. The event attracted a large audience, much publicity, and enjoyed great success, with Irmelin's dancing fairies becoming famous throughout the land.

Nielsen was simultaneously marshalling ideas for different musical genres. Ten years had separated each of his first three symphonies, but the horrifying events of 1914 conspired to precipitate a 'conflict' symphony of great substance soon after *Sinfonia espansiva* (1910–11). While he had been satisfied with his Third Symphony, he believed that his fourth was the breakthrough towards his goal of representing directly through music not a picture or programme from life but the very urge of life itself, its energy and its movement. He told his friends to expect a symphony quite different from its predecessors. The work, *Det uudslukkelige* ('The Inextinguishable'), began his 'organic' period – this word Nielsen used to describe music, especially polyphonic writing and harmonization, which grows out of itself in the process of composition, rather than being first sketched and then fleshed out. Music from this source leads to very intense compositions, since it blossoms from its unique content alone rather than within any premeditated form.

Nielsen, alone and often travelling from 1914 to 1916, wrote letters to close friends in which the genesis of his symphony is revealed as emerging from the core idea of the life force in all its manifestations, biological and human, being transformed by its struggle to survive all obstacles thrown against it. From this emerged the conflicting themes essential to symphonic form. Compared with the contemporary symphonist, Gustav Mahler, who was admired for his exaltation of Romantic feeling, Nielsen preferred to restrict both structure and content to the Classical tradition; intensity was sublimated through the discipline of musical principles. Although usually reluctant to restrict performers or listeners to a narrow interpretation of his music, he confirmed to Thorvald Nielsen that the theme of war had definitely entered the symphony. 'I have an idea about a duel between two kettledrums, something about the war. I've also a subsidiary theme in the first movement, it runs in parallel thirds for some time. It is not quite like me, but it came out that way, so it's going to be like that all the same.'

'Truly, my life has been a stormy sea so far!' So said Nielsen to Röntgen in June 1915, not long after his fiftieth birthday. It may be that without all his recent upheavals and personal upsets the great success of *Sinfonia espansiva* and the Violin Concerto might have brought about a consolidation of Nielsen's style, and given him the contentment enjoyed by his Finnish contemporary, Sibelius, whose works were better known outside his native Finland than were those of Nielsen outside Denmark. Sibelius had recently turned down a professorship at Vienna and had toured England, the United States and Scandinavia. But Nielsen would probably never cease to explore new styles, both in his own compositions and keeping his ear open to the work of others. He reacted with irritation to the music he heard at the 1914 Baltic Music Festival. Having that year relinquished his employment at the Theatre Royal, he accepted appointments to other committees and teaching posts from which vantage point he could influence the future of music and music-making.

*Det uudslukkelige*, his Fourth Symphony, was completed on 14 January 1916 just two weeks before its première in Copenhagen. According to his friend Thorvald Nielsen, 'the audience's tumultuous ovations after the symphony left no doubt that Nielsen had now touched the basic feelings in his overwhelming and powerful musical language. Great as the victory had been with *Espansiva*, this was his decisive triumph. After this gigantic battle his opponents lay felled. Everyone admitted his genius; here was the key to the understanding of Nielsen's music – all his preceding works too.' But not quite! The widening gulf between Nielsen's composing careers – popular songs next to high-brow classical – was commented upon by one colleague. And Thomas Laub, on hearing the Fourth Symphony (which had already been started when he approached Nielsen for his song contributions), openly declared: 'Your music is hellish, and I will not go to Hell!'

Nielsen however knew it to be his best work of recent years, as indicated in a letter to Julius Röntgen. 'I cannot free myself from a number of concepts while I am at work and so it's not really so absurd to talk about it. But I confide only in quite special folk whom I trust … there lies a certain idea behind it, namely that the most elemental nature of music is light, life, and movement which shatters silence

Nielsen photographed in 1916. The score of the Fourth Symphony, which he was in the process of composing, is behind him on the piano.

asunder. Thus it is everything that has the will and desire to live and cannot be held down; that's what I have tried to depict. Not in such a way that I would devalue my art by copying nature, but by attempting to express what lies behind it.' After the symphony had been completed and performed, Nielsen gave his celebrated public explanation of the work.

*The title* Inextinguishable *suggests something which only music itself can express fully: the elementary will of life. Only music can give an abstract expression of life, in contrast to the other arts which must construct models and symbolize. Music solves the problem only by remaining itself, for music is* life *whereas the other arts only* depict *life. Life is unquenchable and inextinguishable; yesterday, today and tomorrow, life was, is, and will be in struggle, conflict, procreation and destruction; and everything returns. Music* is *life, and as such, inextinguishable.*

The symphony's triumph was repeated on 14 April at a portrait concert which also included the Violin Concerto and excerpts from *Saul og David*. At that concert the audience was very enthusiastic, and it was the first time that Nielsen was fully convinced of having an understanding public in Copenhagen, 'and, moreover, a musical public that went to a concert for the sake of art ... For once, I felt I might come to mean something for my country in the future ...'

Early the next year the work was performed in Stockholm, but the Swedes were an uncomprehending audience. It was then performed in cities as diverse as Warsaw, London, Bournemouth, Paris and St Louis. The acclaim it received no doubt owed something to its identification as a war symphony, most obviously expressed in its 'volcanic opening' (to quote Simpson) and in the impressive duel of the two pairs of timpani (which the composer specified should be placed at either side of the orchestra); Nielsen also instructed the players to maintain a menacing character, even in soft passages.

The composer was clearly at the height of his powers, and this is noted by his first biographer, Torben Meyer:

*That he was conscious of his worth as a composer is certain, though he hardly said anything to that effect. His personal address was modest, but distinguished and dignified, and fame and popularity made no difference to it. He did not look at life merely through artistic spectacles; as a man he was too humanly interested in the many-sided struggle for existence for that ... His knowledge of music, literature and art was never used to advertise his intellect; he was not what is usually called 'slick', but it is remarkable how easily (thanks to his charm) he won the confidence of all who came into contact with him.*

After prolonged concentration on major works Nielsen was often troubled by illness, and after completing the Fourth Symphony he developed carbuncles. A skiing trip in Norway with his daughters afforded him the recuperation he needed, and in the autumn of 1916 he began teaching theory and composition at the Conservatoire in Copenhagen. Students expecting such a renowned figure to be intimidating or strict were quickly put at ease when Nielsen told them about his own experiences as a youth, wary of an establishment that was not encouraging to a young novice. But, being aware of his own strength of character, and position within Copenhagen's musical life, Nielsen took care to avoid moulding the individualities of his pupils.

His thoughts returned to the piano after an interval of twenty years. His first period of piano works had stretched from 1890 to 1894–7, with the composition of the *Humoreske-Bagateller*, and these pieces – light and accessible – began where Grieg left off. At the other extreme was the *Symphonic Suite* (1894), which Busoni had christened as positively unpianistic, and which Nielsen himself described as orchestral. Nielsen's second period of piano compositions was dominated by three key works, two composed in 1916 and the third in 1919.

The *Chaconne*, composed in the summer of 1916, was first performed in April 1917 by the Danish pianist Alexander H. Stoffregen. He made some 'improvements' to the score, incorporated in the first printed edition without the composer's approval – Stoffregen, through enriching the chords and including other additional notes, tried to fit the work into more of a late-Romantic tradition. But Nielsen's changes in the pencil and ink autographs are themselves contradictory and ambiguous in intention.

While Nielsen was working on two variations Marie left her studio in order to say to him, 'This won't work, Carl, you must stop! You are overdoing it.' In this she was referring to the work's many dissonances and relentless rhythms. The Danish piano virtuoso Arne Skjold Rasmussen reported this anecdote with approval, and noted the technical difficulties of rendition and the effect of listening to the work: 'it makes so astounding an impact that it takes one's breath away.' The styles and moods of the piece are many and varied, but Nielsen adhered to the chaconne form (a constantly repeated bass theme on which variations are developed). Much of the contrapuntal work has a Baroque feel, yet it is infused with a dramatic movement that is Nielsen alone. The work has been called a true renewal of Danish piano music.

Shortly after completing the *Chaconne*, he devoted himself to the study of Brahms's piano compositions. Sitting at his piano improvising on a Brahms theme one evening, he hit upon a note sequence that he immediately wrote down. This formed the basis of the *Theme with Variations* which was composed in the autumn of 1916 and first performed in November the following year at one of the annual concerts organized by Nielsen for his own works. In the *Theme with Variations* Nielsen's personal style and independence from the nineteenth-century tradition manifested itself in a human, almost eccentric aesthetic – neither mathematical nor in any way Romantic. Rhythm is spontaneous rather than metrically regular, and a successful performance of the work is only possible if the performer communicates its unique and animating 'current' (Nielsen's own word). Irmelin had recoiled at Variations 15, 16 and 17, to which her father had posed the question: 'If I were to strike a sword on a rock so that the sparks flew, wouldn't that be a kind of beauty?'

Unlike the *Chaconne*, in which the variations are joined almost without seams, the variations are so independent in the later work that Nielsen felt obliged to defend his composition to Röntgen. But both works made use of a persistent phrase or rhythm. 'I must also defend myself over the ostinato. To my notions, and my musical ear, the figure is like a constant seeking after a way out, a desperate or comic circling round to find a hole in which to vanish. That hole is G minor, into which it must go and into which it finally does. It is a psychological necessity.' These words illustrate the spontaneous 'human' values which animated Nielsen's music.

Those who view Nielsen's piano compositions in a disparaging light are of the opinion that he was a violinist who used the piano as a

*Following page, the board of the Copenhagen Conservatoire photographed in 1917; from left to right: Godfred Hartmann, Axel Gade, Anton Svendsen, A. P. Weiss and Carl Nielsen*

workbench to compose. This feeling was supported for too long a period of time by neglect and poor playing of Nielsen's piano works – which helped to consolidate his reputation as a symphonist and songwriter. Arne Skjold Rasmussen wrote that 'in spite of Nielsen's inability to give his own compositions an adequate presentation and in spite of breaking new ground he has put his thoughts so effectively in the idiom of the piano that such thoughts do not cross our minds.' France Ellegaard, a pianist born in Paris but whose parents were Danish, saw Nielsen's detachment from piano virtuosity as a great liberation which enabled his imagination to treat the instrument naturally. In her opinion Nielsen's mind was never tied to what his hands could do, and that he wrote entirely the sounds he imagined. The piano works are no more programmatic than the Fourth Symphony, and he explained only to close friends – who would understand the limitations and dangers of analogy – the thoughts he associated with his music.

In the autumn of 1917 the Hungarian violinist Emil Telmányi began writing to Nielsen's younger daughter, Søs (they had first come across each other when Telmányi visited Copenhagen in 1912 when he was aged twenty and she nineteen). They met secretly at Malmö in Sweden, and it was not long before Telmányi proposed to her by telegraph. In the beginning Nielsen belittled the young musician's prospects and opposed the couple's intention to marry, but eventually both parents gave their blessing. In fact, Nielsen's first orchestral work to follow the Fourth Symphony was dedicated to the newly weds, although one imagines that he will not have associated its theme with their romance. *Pan and Syrinx*, taken from Ovid's *Metamorphoses*, is a nature scene for orchestra – comparable to Debussy's impressionist masterpiece *Prélude à l'après-midi d'un faune* which Nielsen had conducted in 1913. Nielsen first had an idea for this music when he was reading Ovid, and he started work on it on the strange peninsula they called Skeiten at Fuglsang.

The score was completed on Søs's wedding day, 6 February 1918, and handed over to her as her gift. The couple, having married in Denmark, then set off on a concert tour that took in Amsterdam and Berlin. After that they travelled on the Orient Express to Telmányi's native Hungary, where they set up home in a small flat. Conditions there were primitive, and there was political turmoil and violence everywhere. Søs was horrified to witness some very brutal scenes, and herself narrowly escaped from armed street bands on one occasion. The next year, when she was twenty-six, the couple decided to return to Copenhagen to live; Telmányi was soon to become his father-in-law's closest friend, supporter and the editor of his music. Nielsen also respected him as a musician of rare talent, and conducted Beethoven's Violin Concerto in Copenhagen with Emil as soloist. Søs proudly wrote of a 'special musical life' that seemed to exist between her husband and her father.

Irmelin was married on 19 December 1919 to a doctor, Eggert Møller, son of a chemist. Nielsen, still separated from his wife Anne Marie, stayed with Irmelin and her husband when he was in Copenhagen or at the Michaelsens' summerhouse in Humlebæk.

In the 1918–19 season Nielsen deputized for Stenhammar in the Göteborg Symphony Orchestra's concerts. At first he took lodgings with an elderly widow, then he moved to a flat at Gøtabergsgaten 2, owned by the Mannheimers, the merchant banking family who had founded the Concert Society in 1905. This family, music lovers who became Nielsen's close friends and supporters, would be prominent during World War II in assisting foreign musicians and refugees.

Telmányi first played Nielsen's Violin Concerto in Göteborg on 11 Feburary 1920 with the composer conducting the city's symphony orchestra. By the time Telmányi retired he had recorded it twice and given at least seventy performances of the work throughout the world. While he was conducting in Göteborg during the 1919–20 season, Nielsen wrote much of his most remarkable composition for piano, the *Suite*, which ended Nielsen's middle phase of piano compositions. Full of powerful and individualistic effects, it was first performed in Copenhagen by Johanne Stockmarr on 14 March 1921. The critics misunderstood its title, *The Luciferan*, and searched throughout the music for demonic elements. Nielsen was in fact referring to Lucifer, the Greek bringer of light.

The work was published with a dedication to Artur Schnabel, but at the publishers' request without the title; instead there was an explanatory preface by Nielsen in which he insisted that every talented artist should have freedom and scope for his own interpretation. That said, he wished the first movement to be rather cold and restrained in tone with a peaceful flowing tempo, the second to be played with the most beautiful tone and subtle use of pedals, the third with transcendental calm and power, and in many places a certain brutal humour. The fourth movement was to have a perfectly chilly, glass-like execution, but with exquisite tone. He described the fifth movement as 'self-evident' and the sixth had a demonic background egging the player on to even stronger and more violent contrasts and more violent accents.

His versatility as a composer had clearly not dissipated his energies. Productivity during the war period had been enormous and concentrated – the direct result of his restless and rootless life. While his most recent key works, especially the Fourth Symphony, had given him some success and satisfaction, he had still to resolve the situation with his wife, and to find some marital, residential and even professional stability.

8

The mature Carl Nielsen,
portrayed in 1922

*What was it like in ancient Greece? Were the
plays of Æschylus reviewed? Did Sophocles have
a good press? Or were their works allowed to
settle naturally in men's minds? Can they have
achieved immortality for the very reason that
they were not 'written up', but struck root and
grew in silence?*

Carl Nielsen, *Living Music*, 1925

# Struggles and Successes 1917–23

Carl Nielsen was constantly being asked to write music for the stage, and by 1917, although dramatic writing came naturally to him, he was not keen to take on theatrical commissions – they had brought him much success but almost always involved him in conflicts and disputes. He nevertheless agreed to write a song for the Icelandic playwright Jóhann Sigurjónsson's *Løgneren* ('The Liar'), which was first performed on 15 February 1918. Suggested by *Njal's Saga*, the play was set in the Viking age and depicts the turbulent displacement of the Norse religions by Christianity. The song is in two parts: first the bard describes two lovers finding happiness; then, following vendettas and intrigues, the young man loses his life, and the girl is left with only her memories.

To counteract the gloom of World War I, the Theatre Royal decided to stage a lavish new production of the vibrant drama *Aladdin*, adapted from the Arabian Nights story by the Danish Romantic poet Adam Oehlenschläger (1779–1850) and first performed by the Theatre Royal in 1839. The actor Johannes Poulsen, who was asked to produce it, was hopeful that Nielsen would agree to write the music – not only was he experienced in providing incidental music but he also had a proven talent for writing music of a joyous and festive nature. The theatre's director, Johannes Nielsen, a friend of Carl's, knew all about his bitter experiences with the theatre. But despite framing his request to the composer in a poem, the commission was declined. Nielsen suffered a certain inhibition whenever he came anywhere near the theatre, and had even refused to see its production of the play *Fatherland*, to which he had contributed.

*Ten years ago a request from the Theatre Royal to write music would have been a great joy and encouragement ... but then the art of music was still surrounded by a certain splendour through the personality of Johan Svendsen ... I have already tried to write music for* Aladdin *... but every time I think about the theatre I lose enthusiasm ...*

Eventually the new production of *Aladdin* captivated Nielsen's imagination and he relented. Although the subject inspired some of his most glorious and popular music, his misgivings that the theatre would continue to create difficulties would prove to be justified.

The composer's first difficulty was to complete enough work in time for the rehearsals of the corps de ballet – he had only received the text in the summer of 1918. He was also concerned that at the time he started work no agreement had been reached concerning his fee. He wrote to his wife (for even when separated they continued to champion each other's artistic career): 'I want to be well paid, considering my name and my age.' During his summer holiday at his recently purchased summer house, 'Finis Terrae', at the sea-front town of Skagen, Nielsen began to work furiously while the theatre pressed him to deliver the scores. A pupil of his, Nancy Dalberg, helped him to produce the score. Even so, progress was slow, and in January 1919 Nielsen wrote to Stenhammar that he had been 'going through a frightful amount of work' on *Aladdin*, and although it was growing incessantly, to three, four hundred pages of score, he was still not

The summer house 'Finis Terrae' at Skagen, the most northerly point in Denmark; here Nielsen could work away from the distractions of Copenhagen.

finished. At this time, in his summer house, which was quickly a
favourite retreat, he was adding the final touches to his *Suite* for piano.

Nielsen was determined to capture as much of the authentic spirit
of Oriental music as possible. His Oriental Festival March, Dance
of the Morning Mist and The Market in Ispahan seem hardly to
betray the fingerprints of the Danish composer; all the music in fact
has an authentic Oriental feel. He had remembered his visit to
Constantinople in 1903, when he had witnessed dancing dervishes,
and had taken time and extra care to immerse himself in the mood,
and also familiarize himself with the text that his music would
faithfully serve.

Four solo songs were written for the second part of the score at a
point where the drama concentrates more on its leading characters,
but most of the score consists of orchestral music, to accompany the
processions and the dances. Seven of these orchestral pieces were
published separately to form the *Aladdin Suite*, which immediately
became a popular concert piece. Nielsen had created this concert suite
before *Aladdin*'s opening night in the sad realization that the Theatre

Nielsen's visit to
Constaninople in 1903 –
here he is photographed in
fez with Ove Jørgensen –
enabled him to capture the
authentic feel of oriental
music when he came to write
the music for *Aladdin*.

Royal was spoiling the effect of his work by editing the score and changing the order of items without his consent. Following his dismay at the première of Part I on 15 February 1919 (plans for the musical drama had grown to enormous proportions, and it was staged over two evenings), Nielsen quickly issued a statement:

> *In previous information given about the performance of* Aladdin, *it has been stated that I composed the music. On account of the placing and restrictions of the orchestra, and because of the manner in which the production has generally used my compositions, I must disclaim any responsibility for the musical side of* Aladdin. *As a result I have written to the Theatre Royal ... indicating that I did not want my name displayed upon the programme or posters ... and that only on this condition would I refrain from withdrawing my music.*

No response from the theatre seemed to be forthcoming, but the management eventually complied with Nielsen's request. This meddling with his work was, however, the final rock upon which any plans Nielsen may have had to renew Scandinavian opera were dashed.

He had already conducted an orchestral suite of six excerpts from *Aladdin* at a concert in Stockholm on 6 February which had confirmed the music's powerful effect; and as a result of this, the critics, having attended its première, supported the composer's disclaimer. The reviewer in *Theatre* wrote:

> *In these dances Carl Nielsen's remarkable capacity for characterization and colourful illustration scored a remarkable triumph ... The composer's resentment was justified. What happened, for example, to the whole effect of the superbly scored music for the market scene in Ispahan? All those colourful and rhythmically distinct sounds finally blending in motley Oriental confusion? We must hope some day that Carl Nielsen will again give the public a chance to hear the* Aladdin *music it could not hear at the theatre.*

The first performance of the music would have to wait until one of Nielsen's Concert Society evenings in Copenhagen, on 12 November 1925, when the twenty-six pieces were conducted by the composer in their original order. *Aladdin* was a major accomplishment, and it is

Nielsen's most colourful dramatic music, despite its neglect for many years following its first production.

Travelling became easier at the end of World War I. Nielsen, who would use Copenhagen as his base for the rest of his life, from 1920 onwards travelled across Europe where audiences were increasingly eager to hear his music. One encounter, with the Hungarian composer Béla Bartók in 1920 in Budapest, was not free from acrimony. The tale goes that Bartók asked Nielsen what he thought of his music, specifically whether he thought it to be sufficiently modern. Bartók's doubts as to his own music's modernity and Nielsen's contempt for Bartók's music showed neither composer in a good light. Telmányi's alternative account seems more reliable, as he was an eye-witness to the event, and also a native Hungarian. The 'confrontation' took place at a tea party hosted by Ernő Dohnányi and attended by various musical dignitaries. Bartók's String Quartet No. 2, written three years earlier, was played. Telmányi's retelling of the event is that the question put to Nielsen by Bartók was whether he considered the music of the quartet to be sufficiently modern, and that the essence of Nielsen's reply was that modernism was not a measure of musical quality. Conflicting versions of this story then dragged on for years afterwards through the columns of musical journals.

In Paris that year Nielsen met his old friend Busoni. His estranged wife Anne Marie also agreed to meet him there, and the couple revisited places they had not returned to since their first meeting in the French city thirty years before. This romantic reunion, after some five years of separation, revealed their mutual desire for a reconcilia-tion, but despite this apparently happy meeting, Nielsen travelled on alone to Barcelona to join his patron, the industrialist Carl Michaelsen, and Nancy Dalberg, on a tour of Spain. The friendliness and honest character of the Spanish people made a strong and lasting impression upon Nielsen.

On his way back to Denmark he attended a music festival in Amsterdam where he was impressed by the Dutch conductor Willem Mengelberg and his orchestra. He was also pleased with a performance there of his Sonata for Violin and Piano No. 2 given by Telmányi and Schnabel. When finally back in Copenhagen, the composer informed his daughters of the respect with which he was increasingly being received all over Europe – and even in places where his music had not to his knowledge been performed.

During this trip Nielsen had completed a commission for the Theatre Royal which he had accepted for patriotic reasons only. After World War I a majority of citizens in north Schleswig voted to reunite with Denmark after fifty-six years of German rule (that had begun with the war of 1864). To celebrate this event the theatre commissioned the author Helge Rode to write a festive play, *Moderen* ('The Mother[land]'). His work, like a fairy-tale set in modern times, was an allegory about the return of a kidnapped daughter. It inspired Nielsen to write light and catchy yet moving patriotic songs that have outlived the stilted and ephemeral play, first performed on 30 January 1921. Two of the best known are *Min pige er saa lys som rav* ('My Girl is as Fair as Amber'), and *Saa bittert var mit hjerte* ('So Bitter was My Heart'). Some delightful instrumental pieces written for *Moderen* are also regularly performed and appear on many recordings. The historical reunification inspired other Danish writers: the south Jylland poet H. Lorenzen wrote *Gry* ('Dawn'), which Nielsen set to music. The composer had also composed the melody for Hostrup's *The Lark*, written after the territories were lost in 1864, which depicted the eagle in opposition to the dove.

Nielsen continued to travel widely, striving to define and accomplish his objectives in several genres. His reputation abroad, however, was never to be enhanced by his songs or his music for the stage; his other works were sufficient to maintain his now high profile. In 1921 he wrote from Helsinki to his wife on the occasion of a performance of *Hymnus amoris* and the E flat String Quartet: 'Sibelius was beside himself over it, and the ovations ... are getting quite tiring.' Still separated from Anne Marie, Nielsen suffered periods of deep despair and rootlessness. His close musical friends could not help him, and personal friends were not compensation for the marriage he badly wished to reinstate.

During January 1922 Carl Nielsen was finally reunited with Anne Marie in Berlin. On the fifteenth of the month they returned to Copenhagen together, having been reconciled on the very day that he signed off his masterpiece, the Fifth Symphony, begun the year before. This symphony drove him much harder than any of his previous works. It was begun at Michaelsen's home at Højbo in Humlebæk, continued at Nielsen's summer house in Skagen, then over July and August 1921 at Damgaard, the Jylland home of his friend Charlotte

Marie Trap de Thygeson. Each night he worked on his symphony well into the early hours until putting it aside to compose *Fynsk foraar* ('Springtime on Fyn'). Rehearsals for its first peformance on 1 September were about to begin.

*Fynsk foraar*, Nielsen's most popular choral work, depicts the coming of spring in Fyn, the region of Nielsen's birth, and it is a perfect musical complement to *Min fynske barndom*, the rural autobiography that Nielsen was to write only five years later. *Fynsk foraar* is written from an uncomplicated child-like perspective, and can easily be performed by good amateur performers. The work in fact had its origin in a Danish Choral Society competition for a text which Nielsen had agreed then to set to music. The winner of the competition was Aage Berntsen, a doctor and poet from Fyn, whose politician father had sponsored Nielsen's entry to the Conservatoire in Copenhagen.

Although the subject was very close to Nielsen's heart, the composition of the work had an inauspicious beginning. The composer was so totally engrossed in the Fifth Symphony that he put aside thoughts of other work – to the extent of mislaying Berntsen's text which had been in his care for some time. Eventually, and to his great relief, he found the manuscript, which had slipped behind a drawer in his study back home in Frederiksholm Kanal. The music for *Fynsk foraar* was thus written in a space of only two weeks.

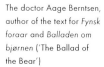

The doctor Aage Berntsen, author of the text for *Fynsk foraar* and *Balladen om bjørnen* ('The Ballad of the Bear')

Framed by two choral sections describing the life of the island community, a series of episodes depicts the thoughts and feelings of various people on the island. For everyone the end of winter brings renewed hope and excitement. At the centre of the work is the charming song of the blind musician (*Den blinde spillemand*) which brings to mind the character of Blind Anders who played in the village band with Nielsen's father. The sounds of the blind man's clarinet to which the children are dancing are quite different from the sinister voice of the instrument as it is depicted in the symphony composed at the same time. The première of *Fynsk foraar*, on 8 July 1922, was an event of national importance attended by the King and Queen of Denmark. The large Market Hall of Odense was filled to its capacity of 8,000 people, to hear Georg Høeberg conduct a choir of 800 drawn from all parts of the country.

Nielsen's Fifth Symphony is his masterpiece: the summation and clarification of much of his prior art. Like the First Symphony, it has no title. Those of the intervening symphonies, *De fire temperamenter*, *Sinfonia espansiva* and *Det uudslukkelige*, were, according to Nielsen, 'really only various names for the same thing that only music can ultimately express: the passive forces in contrast to the active'. Although the pencil manuscript contains the words 'Vague forces – alert forces', Nielsen withheld a title because he did not want the symphony to be limited in its scope by a general public who would tend to clutch too firmly to verbal clues. To Dolleris, Nielsen described the fundamental opposition as 'dream' versus 'deeds', and to Hugo Seligman as between 'vegetative' and 'active' states of mind. Sir Simon Rattle broke the mould by perceptively describing the Fifth Symphony rather than the Fourth as being Nielsen's War Symphony. While the subject of both is survival in the face of struggle, the Fourth Symphony concerns unwitting life energies and the Fifth forces that are organized and specifically human – there are clashes between good and evil, with both formative and antagonistic, creative and destructive elements. The scale of the Fifth Symphony is unprecedented, and the traditional symphonic four-movement structure is abandoned in favour of one in two broad parts.

Instead of plunging immediately into a torrent of orchestral energies awaiting resolution, the symphony opens with a mysterious representation of the void, the earth without form as it were. Simpson

The first performance of *Fynsk foraar* at the Market Hall of Odense, July 1922. More than 800 singers and musicians performed to an audience of 8,000.

Wilhelm Furtwängler
rehearses Nielsen's Fifth
Symphony in Frankfurt,
1927. 'I certainly know that
it is neither quite so easy to
place nor so simple to play,'
was Nielsen's comment on
the symphony.

explained in a sleeve note that the movement begins 'in outer space.
A wave-like viola line appears from nowhere, as if one were suddenly
made aware of time as a dimension. Against this passing of time
shadowy shapes begin to form; they are unclear, and create problems,
as if seen by a dawning consciousness unable yet to recognize objects,
and finding them vaguely frightening.' Two themes are introduced,
both of which are relentless, insidious and ultimately disruptive of the
first part of the symphony, leading to the contribution of the snare-
drummer who is directed by the composer to improvise 'as if at all
costs to stop the progress of the music'. In this task he is assisted by
cymbals, triangle and tambourine – percussion instruments which had
featured little in Nielsen's earlier symphonies and are conspicuous by
their absence even in the crescendos of this symphony's Part Two.

In Part One the confrontation arises from innocent themes that
become totally destructive: the violence of the symphony is disturbing
because it is deliberately and self-consciously evil, well-orchestrated
in a political sense rather than being a spontaneous eruption of
terror. In the wildest parts, the music is distinctly martial; a heavy
ostinato passed from timpani to pizzicato lower strings is a persistent
rhythm that turns into what Simpson describes as 'the tick of a
monstrous clock'.

In Part Two, an allegro containing two contrasting fugues, the
listener inhabits a world reborn, at first calm but a world which

produces new struggles and menacing dangers. It seems as though
Nielsen, who never lived to witness the discovery of nuclear energy, is
no longer certain that life is inextinguishable, as suggested in his
previous symphony. The Fifth was the culmination Nielsen had aimed
for in his Fourth Symphony: the European war had not been pursued
to its bitter end but had stopped before all evil had been rooted out.
The Fourth was too optimistic, in its portrayal of the triumph of good
over evil. Its successor heralds the coming of a second European war,
but the more mysterious second part defies cerebral analysis (Simpson
hesitated over analysing Part Two, feeling that it either needed very
deep analysis or, on the contrary, to be described in the fewest possible
words): it transports the listener through the depths or above the
heights of more standard musical perceptions.

Of this symphony Nielsen commented that, 'It has been said that
my symphony is not like my earlier ones. I cannot see that myself, but
maybe that's so. I certainly know that it is neither quite so easy to
place nor as simple to play. We have had many rehearsals of it. Some
have suggested that now Arnold Schoenberg might as well pack up his
discords as mine are worse. But I certainly hope that they are not.'

The Fifth Symphony was completed while Nielsen was conducting
in Göteborg, and first performed only two weeks later on 24 January
1922 at the Concert Society in Copenhagen. It was dedicated to
his friends the Michaelsens, whose country home had provided the
composer with a refuge from his domestic problems and other interruptions. Michaelsen, an industrialist with a highly developed
musical sense, was aware of the symphony's worth, and advised
Nielsen to reject Hansen's terms. Michaelsen then started up his own
music publishing business, Hans Borups Musikforlag, and printed
his friend's new symphony himself, for which Nielsen received the
sum of 2,000 DKr, two or three times his expectation.

After its Danish première the Fifth Symphony was performed in
Göteborg, Berlin, then in Stockholm on 20 January 1924 when some
of the audience walked out mid-performance, protesting at the
cacophonous effect of the snare drum. But this was not gratuitous
noise – it is a threatening element delayed until late in Part One
because only at a certain stage in evolution, according to Simpson, do
opposing forces crystallize: it reflects the stage that the social evolution
of man has reached, and illustrates a conflict far more frightening than

man's earlier war in the jungle. Dmitry Shostakovich was later to use a similar effect in his *Leningrad* Symphony.

Nielsen acknowledged no limit to his own energies and disclosed that he had worked regularly on the symphony from ten in the morning until five the next morning without fatigue. He immediately started work on a quintet for wind instruments, and, in the spring of 1922, the reaction to such a punishing workload came in his most serious attack of angina to date. Not only was this disease physically incapacitating – and ultimately fatal – but it must have dampened Nielsen's usually cheerful disposition.

Despite being one of Nielsen's later works, the popular Wind Quintet is one of the composer's most accessible compositions. It seems neither modern nor archaic, and has instead a timeless and universal feel to it, heralding a new phase of compositional style. In some respects anticipating Stravinsky's neo-classicism, Nielsen's music of this phase was more abstract, analytical and strict in its adherence to Classical structures. The origin of this major chamber

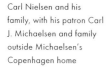

Carl Nielsen and his family, with his patron Carl J. Michaelsen and family outside Michaelsen's Copenhagen home

piece, the first since the string quartets, is well documented. One evening in 1921 Nielsen had telephoned his friend Christian Christiansen and had heard in the background four members of the Copenhagen Wind Quintet rehearsing Mozart's Sinfonia Concertante for wind instruments. The quality of the sound over the telephone was obviously poor, but Nielsen was none the less curious and he was soon participating at the rehearsal.

A few months after this he hinted to the oboist of the group, Svend Christian Felumb, that he was at work on something new and that the ensemble would become its dedicatees. The Copenhagen Quintet are significant in this regard because Nielsen set out to capture their personalities in his work. (Two of the five were later to be immortalized in concertos: for both clarinettist Aage Oxenvad, noted for his irascibility, and the fastidious flautist Gilbert Jespersen, replacing Paul Hagemann as the quintet's flautist, Nielsen was to write a concerto that would portray each one through the breath of his instrument.)

Again, Nielsen worked extremely long hours on the quintet, but with great enjoyment. It was first played on 30 April 1922 by its dedicatees at the Mannheimers' home in Göteborg on the occasion of Lisa Mannheimer's birthday. Its first public performance, on 9 October that year, was a resounding success. *Politiken* proclaimed it 'an important work from beginning to end', and *Socialdemokraten* observed that the solo variations for bassoon and horn were quite astonishing, and that nothing like it had been written before. The character studies of the musical instruments, the chamber sonorities, and its timeless style made the work uncontroversial but eloquent, accessible yet admired by the buffs.

The first movement is in a Classical sonata form, with the main theme repeated before development; the second is a minuet reminiscent of Baroque suites; the third is a remarkable set of eleven variations on Nielsen's melody to the hymn, *Min Jesus, lad mit hjerte faa* ('My Jesus make my heart to love Thee'). By 1922 this tune was so well known in Denmark that its use here must have carried some significance. Writing a programme note in which he expressed his role (in the third person, with customary modesty), the composer said: 'The theme for these variations is the tune of one of Carl Nielsen's spiritual songs, which is here made the basis of a number of variations, now gay and grotesque, now elegiac and solemn, ending with the theme itself, simply and gently expressed.'

In this third movement the individual expression of each of the five instruments in variations is revealed in the variations, whether playing solo or in ensemble. Nielsen told the horn player, Hans Sørensen, that he imagined him standing up on a hill blowing so that he could be heard in every nook and cranny, and the composer noted on the pencil autograph in the Carl Nielsen Archive (but not on the printed score), 'Unless done with naïve abandonment to the atmosphere of nature it's no good.' Sørensen was of plain and down-to-earth character, with a military band training. Nielsen approached Felumb to ask if it would be possible to replace the oboe with the more sombre cor anglais, an idea probably suggested by Berlioz's *Symphonie fantastique* which Nielsen had just conducted in Copenhagen, and in which Felumb had played the long and lovely solo on that instrument.

*Balladen om bjørnen* ('The Ballad of the Bear'), composed in 1923, is one of the few Lieder that Nielsen ever wrote for professional recital, as distinct from his popular songs. Of the small number, this song is his most successful, and Nielsen himself was 'reasonably satisfied with the work'. Irmelin considered it very dramatic, yet its harsh dissonance (far from the simplicity of the popular songs) aptly expresses the anguish of a feud between a she-bear who inflicts a savage revenge on the man who killed her cubs. Nielsen had often spoken of his fascination for the poetry of the Swede C. J. L. Almquist (1793–1866), and he persuaded Aage Berntsen to adapt Almquist's complex wilderness saga of the she-bear from the *Book of the Rose*.

In January 1923 the master of dissonance, Arnold Schoenberg, visited Copenhagen to conduct a concert of his own works. Nielsen met him, and although it was a cordial meeting, the Danish composer respected his Austrian colleague for his personal integrity but did not admire his recent works in which tonality had been completely abandoned. By this time Nielsen's own opinions on music held such force in Copenhagen that the next generation of Danish composers was relatively isolated from the influences of their European contemporaries. Bartók and Stravinsky, who visited Copenhagen in July 1924, however, did influence the younger Danish composers who sought to avoid both Nielsen's 'humanism' and Gade's 'Romanticism', even though it was well known that Nielsen, now firmly at the helm of Danish music, did not admire the music of either.

In April 1923 Nielsen had been invited to conduct the London Symphony Orchestra in a programme of his works, an event that would constitute his British debut. He travelled to London with Søs and Emil, who was giving a recital in the Aeolian Hall on 27 June, five days after the concert of his father-in-law's works. For Emil's recital Nielsen was busy on a new work for solo violin, the *Prelude and Theme with Variations*. Its formal structure closely follows the finale of the Wind Quintet, and the openings of both preludes start with a dissonant D flat. But while the Quintet movement can still be analysed in terms of tonal harmony, the new work for solo violin is Nielsen's first response to the challenge of atonality. It was completed after his arrival in London. The LSO concert at the Queen's Hall was to comprise the Fourth Symphony, *Pan and Syrinx*, the Violin Concerto and excerpts from *Maskarade*. At the first rehearsal Nielsen climbed on to the podium and established an immediate rapport with the players, with his amusing 'Gentlemen, I am glad to see you. I hope I am also glad to *hear* you!' The concert was patronized by Queen Alexandra, who was the daughter of Christian IX of Denmark, and Nielsen was invited to take tea with her at Marlborough House. He discovered that he had forgotten to bring his dark suit and so borrowed Telmányi's, trying to keep his hand over the top button which he could not do up. All seemed well until Alexandra's sister, the Empress Dagmar of Russia, joined the company, and Nielsen was

The daughters of King Christian IX of Denmark: Queen Alexandra (centre) and Empress Dagmar of Russia (right), with Princess Victoria of England (left). Nielsen took tea with Alexandra and Dagmar on his only visit to Britain in June 1923.

Nielsen pictured next to
his Renault K3377. He called
the car, a gift from C. J.
Michaelsen, 'the sentry-box'
because of its tall, box-like
proportions.

asked to lead both ladies into tea. In doing so the undone button was
exposed but luckily it drew forth no comment. In his room in
Cranston's Ivanhoe Hotel in Bloomsbury Street, Telmányi was
anxiously awaiting the return of his suit which he needed for his
evening recital. A happy Carl Nielsen had however a queen on one
arm and an empress on the other!

Excessive work had taken its toll on Nielsen's health since
completing the Fifth Symphony, and in 1924, because of his heart
condition, the composer was ordered to give up riding. He was
bitterly disappointed and told friends that he did not wish to live if
he were physically incapacitated. But things were looking up when
Michaelsen visited his friend at the Copenhagen Conservatoire,
took him to the window, and handed him the keys to K3377 – the
composer's first car. Nielsen became a keen motorist and was often to
be seen driving around the country in his Renault (or the Sentry Box,
as he called it, its tall cabin forming an L-shape). But his driving was
notorious, and it was fortunate indeed that no one ever got in his way.
As he explained, 'When the police themselves teach you how to drive,
you can knock down Satan without compunction.' He was now
able to travel by car from Copenhagen to Skagen in north Jylland,
although observers were surprised that the vehicle survived the rain
and bad roads. Once, when driving through Fyn with Søs as his
passenger, Nielsen asked her to have a look and tell him what seemed
to be running across the field. It was in fact one of the car's wheels,
which had worked itself free, but the car still worked perfectly well
with one wheel absent! Nielsen often gave lifts to strangers, one of
whom was a down-and-out who requested to be dropped off to visit
his friends in prison. Søs's mother, so her daughter said, adhered more
to conventions than her father. Yet in their respective lives and art,
it is perhaps more accurate to say that each was bold and eccentric,
but in differing ways, resulting in both artistic and domestic tensions
and creativity.

In 1924 Nielsen was approaching his sixtieth birthday. And yet
in contrast to his contemporary Sibelius who had just written the
last symphony he was to write, Nielsen was just entering the most
energetic compositional period of his life.

9

A gathering at the Göteborg
home of bank director
Herman Mannheimer i.
1923. In the back row aɾᴇ
Harald and Birgit
Fürstenberg, Herman
Mannheimer, Barbro
Tadros, Emil Telmányi and
Anna Lisa Mannheimer.
Anne Marie Telmányi,
Henriette Magnus and Carl
Nielsen are at the front.

*If, in common with architecture, [music] can
proclaim nothing definite and cannot, like
poetry, painting, and sculpture, convey information about what we call nature and reality,
it can, more than any of these, illumine,
emphasize, suggest, and clarify ... the most
elementary feelings and most heavily charged
emotions ... This may explain the riddle of why
music, more than any other art, relentlessly
reveals its origin, the composer.*

Carl Nielsen, *Living Music*, 1925

# A Riddle Wrapped in an Enigma 1924-6

The final seven years of Nielsen's life were his most creative despite his declining health and ever increasing claims on his time. His youthful looks vanished very rapidly after 1925, the year which marked his sixtieth birthday. Newly whitened hair gave him an air of dignity that befitted his status, and yet it worried his friends. Now, however, he was back together with Marie and living in her artist's state town-house; his daughters were married and his son lived in the country as a gardener. As the waves on Nielsen's 'stormy sea' settled, he looked back on his long struggle to establish his artistic goals, pondering the significance of his life's work. At times he believed that he had come to have sufficient admirers in Denmark and abroad, and that what he had established musically was at last appreciated and could be built on.

The popular choral work *Fynsk foraar*, which he had composed in July and August 1921, had been biographically retrospective. Stylistically progressive in its dissonance and angular rhythms, yet popular and accessible, it was a study from nature, authentically flavoured by Nielsen's own happy childhood – eighteen years of happiness according to his rose-tinted memory. Moving on to consider the four decades which separated these childhood years from their musical reflection, each of Nielsen's symphonies definitely reveal the outlook of its creator even if they are not manifestly biographical. His first was an assertion of his strength as a young composer. Ten years elapsed before the second (*De fire temperamenter*, 1901–2) expressed Nielsen's understanding of the varieties and extremities of human nature. Another decade passed, and at the peak of Nielsen's personal and artistic life the *Sinfonia espansiva* celebrated his domestic bliss and his joy from honest and fruitful labour. Within three years this tranquillity was but a happy memory: Europe was at war, Nielsen's marriage had collapsed, and he had been ousted from his position in Copenhagen's musical establishment. His Fourth Symphony (*Det uudslukkelige*, 1915–16) unleashed a ferocious conflict

– including the remarkable duel of the timpani – but it was a conflict viewed from the standpoint of Nielsen's deep-seated optimism. This optimism he expressed by presenting through his music an indestructible life-force; in the cyclical order of things there is destruction but then renewal. The Fifth Symphony also expressed life's struggle, but at a more organized level of civilization; it is pessimistic in its conclusion of the outcome of a planetary struggle of rival factions.

While still at work on his Fifth Symphony, Nielsen wrote that it was the most difficult task he had set himself, and that the next time he would 'select an "easy" style to amuse myself, and, I hope, others'. His next symphony was optimistically titled *Sinfonia semplice* ('Simple Symphony') and it was begun at his seaside home in Skagen during the summer of 1924; his work on it, however, was put aside until his creative currents emerged to indicate to him the nature of the third and fourth movements. Consciously, or otherwise, the eventual symphony was to be Nielsen's most biographical and least optimistic symphonic document; and as such, it was not initially well received.

During the Sixth Symphony's gestation Nielsen continued to give much to the future of Danish song. His major contributions to Bishop Grundtvig's Folk High School Movement had been contained in the first edition of the *Folkehøjskolens melodibog* ('The Folk High School Melody Book'), first published in 1922. These folk high schools (not attended by the composer) were part of an important Danish movement which from the late nineteenth-century offered adult education and also the development of practical skills. In 1924 Nielsen contributed forty-four songs and the foreword to *Sangbogen Danmark* ('The Danish Songbook'), a collection of simple songs for pleasure at school and home which quickly became a standard text; two years later a revised and enlarged edition benefited from eighteen more of Nielsen's songs. It is through songs like these, rather than the symphonies, that all Danish people are familiar with the music, if not the name, of Carl Nielsen. The composer also published light-hearted Christmas carols seasonally or in small collections, and in 1925 wrote Four Jylland Songs, which admirably caught the regional dialect. They were set to texts by Aage Berntsen, author of *Fynsk foraar* and son of Nielsen's principal benefactor.

Work on the Sixth Symphony was interrupted by the celebration of his sixtieth birthday on 9 June 1925. This day was declared a national

Nielsen and family on the morning of his sixtieth birthday, 9 June 1925. From left to right: Irmelin, Anne Marie Carl-Nielsen, Eggert Møller, Carl Nielsen, Hans Børge, Anne Marie Telmányi, Maren Hansen and Emil Telmányi. The dressing-gown Nielsen wears was a birthday present from Irmelin.

holiday, and the festivities in Copenhagen were recorded by his younger daughter, Søs, and by his friend, Thorvald Nielsen. It was a sunny day and in Nielsen's garden his favourite blue cornflowers and big red poppies were in full bloom. He awoke to the sounds of a brass band and, robed in a purple silk dressing gown which had been a gift from Irmelin, he appeared in his garden where he was photographed with his family. That day he was to become a Knight Commander of the second Grade of the Dannebrog (the Danish flag) and the stream of people to the house bearing congratulations and gifts seemed never-ceasing. At one point Nielsen retired to rest and his wife left the house on some errand. She returned to find an irritated Swedish Foreign Minister solemnly pacing outside their door, trying to present Nielsen with his nation's distinguished Order. Maren contined to be notorious in allowing no one to disturb her master.

At the request of the publishers Martins Forlag, *Living Music*, a collection of Nielsen's essays on musical theory, had been published a few days earlier. These essays allow a rare insight into Nielsen's musical philosophy – as generally he was not inclined to explain or codify his creative approach. In Denmark *Living Music* rapidly became a kind of New Testament for the country's composers although – perhaps true to scriptures and artistic genius alike – his writings were sometimes contradictory. He often seemed opposed to elements of his own music (cautioning against mixing the arts yet well aware of literary and visual influences on his music).

In the evening a gala concert was held in the Tivoli. First on the programme was the *Little Suite for Strings*, Nielsen's first major première performed again in the same venue after thirty-seven years; Peder Møller followed with Nielsen's Violin Concerto, and in the second half Nielsen conducted his Symphony No. 5 and *Fynsk foraar*. The applause seemed to be without end and it resounded like thunder when the composer was presented with two giant laurel wreaths. There then followed a lavish banquet at Nimbs Restaurant. When Nielsen arrived at the restaurant with his wife, his three children, Maren and his brother Albert who had come from Chicago, they were received to yet more enthusiastic applause while the band struck up the march from *Aladdin*. Later the band entertained the dining crowd with some pieces from *Maskarade*. Vilhelm Andersen gave a speech in which he described Danish culture to be a result of the interplay of characteristics of people from Fyn, Jylland and Sjælland: 'The man from Fyn has both patience and ability. He can both play the violin and make it himself.' Then Olfert Jespersen, the band-leader who had found the teenage prodigy in a basement tavern in Odense, gave a few words, and the two men warmly embraced, unable to conceal their emotion. More speeches followed and much laughter. But Carl Nielsen was serious as he rose to give his reply. He described his childhood in Fyn, how he grew up in poverty, but with parents whom he perceived as perfect. 'My mother always said to me, "You should always endeavour to carry out your work to the best of your ability, and don't forget that Hans Christian Andersen was poor like you."' These words, Nielsen said, he had always kept in mind. And he protested that the honours he received were far too much: what he had done as a musician, he had done with delight as a labour of love.

In 1925 Carl's brother Albert returned from Chicago; he and Carl are photographed outside their childhood cottage.

Many others might have done the same but he had been fortunate
enough to have had the time and favourable circumstances. When
labouring over a composition he would never say to himself that the
work would be outstanding, he merely tried to carry out the work as
best he could. Nielsen's ascent from obscurity to international renown
has been the central element in many of his biographies, but to the
composer his background and how it determined his creativity was as
inconsequential as the recognition of his music was vital.

Nielsen left the restaurant to greet a torchlight procession, heralded
by the sounds of a brass band: musicians and students had assembled
and marched from the Riding Grounds of Christianborg Castle
singing some of Nielsen's patriotic songs. After some appreciative
words from the singer Poul Wiedemann, Nielsen spoke to the
assembled people:

*I thank you for all your torches, which bring warmth and light. I take
them to express that, in your opinion, I have something of this in me. I
do not know it myself. But I tell you that there are many, many talents in
this country that are not given a chance to develop. All of you have some
of these faculties in you. And I want to tell you that I have never composed anything so beautiful as what I have seen here tonight. Should I
ever be able to express in music what this is, then listen to me. My dear
friends! We are all made of the same stuff, all of us have life's faculties in
us, if only we could use these faculties. I myself am so very little, and it is
by chance that I became the man I am.*

Shortly afterwards he confided to Thorvald Nielsen: 'Oh yes, now
they praise me, but it doesn't matter now that I can do whatever I like,
but the many years in my youth when it might have been a help for
me – never mind ...' Nielsen characteristically dismissed the thought
with a gesture of his hand, but later in the year he gave an outspoken
interview to *Politiken*, in which he said that he would chase all artistic
whims from his head if he were able to live his life again. He would
learn a trade, or other useful work, in which he could see results.

*What human satisfaction it must give when a man can shut up his
shop or his workshop in the evening, knowing that he has done some good,
honest work, and will get a reasonable reward for it ... But for the artist*

*it is just the opposite. The greater his idealism and the intensity he puts
into his work, the less the pecuniary reward. The public just doesn't
understand it, it has no success ... The businessman reaps both honour
and pecuniary advantages. The artist, never the latter, and sometimes not
even the former.*

These comments were considered bitter and uncharacteristic, but
they were consistent with the advice he had always given others since
the beginning of his own career as a composer.

During the same month he conducted the fiftieth performance
of *Maskarade* and purchased a larger car, a Morris, which he enthusiastically took across the country and abroad. After a brief curative
holiday at Menton with his wife, who had caught a cough in her
chilly studio, Nielsen returned home to work on the Sixth Symphony.
This time, the difficulties he faced in the composition of the work
were resolved by an interval of contemplation rather than long hours
of concentration. The symphony's first movement had begun in
search of a simple, timeless, purely musical apogee. But the second
movement became a humorous jibe at the direction in which modern
music was going (which in turn prompted Nielsen into a retrospective
view of his own contribution). The third and fourth movements, like
all great art, held their secrets for a long time; they contain moments
of bitterness and anguish if not despair, but these emotions are briefly
expressed within a context which might be considered realistic or
resigned rather than pessimistic. All this, however, was far from
Nielsen's initial plan.

On 12 August 1924 he wrote to Søs, cautioning her to discuss the
matter with no one else, but asking her to seek Emil's opinion on 'a
whole new symphony of an entirely idyllic character ... outside all
tastes and fashions, only fine and heartfelt musical devotion in
sounds in the same manner as the old *a cappella* musicians but with
the resources of our times.' On 22 October Nielsen confided to
Michaelsen: 'I am getting along well with my new symphony. As far
as I can see it will on the whole be of a different character than my
others: more charming, smooth ... but it's not good to say anything, as
I know nothing about the currents that can appear during the voyage.'
Nielsen had, as never before, discussed the process of composition, yet
he also concealed as never before its contents which in any case he

admitted he could not foresee. The Sixth Symphony was not sketched
and fleshed out. The first movement was completed by 20 November
1924 and the (very brief) second movement the following January
but, having posed the question of where music was going, Nielsen was
then left in uncharted territories, not knowing how to proceed or
what would emerge. But in an interview in April 1925 he stated that
he was still working on his Sixth Symphony, and that it would be 'so-
called absolute music'.

The extent to which Nielsen's previous symphonies contained
extra-musical ideas is debatable but biographically crucial, as it
establishes or otherwise denies a connection between an artist's life
and work. Nielsen said that music expressed matters which other arts
could not. In discussing his Fourth Symphony he had used his famous
motto that music *was* life, and explained that it did not merely imitate
natural phenomena but was capable of representing the movement
and urges which underlie what becomes visible or apparent, ideas that
are even more deeply buried in the Sixth Symphony. Late in the
twentieth century most listeners can enjoy the musical content of the
work without needing to find meanings, parodies and parallels.

On 5 December 1925 the score was completed, and only six days
later the symphony was given its first performance in Copenhagen
under the composer's baton. At the time of the première Nielsen still
refrained from discussing the completed work. In a newspaper
interview a few days before the concert, when asked what he depicted
in the new symphony, Nielsen responded with, 'Only purely musical
matters.' And in another interview dating from the same time he
spoke only of his aim of arriving at the greatest simplicity possible.

Those who might have expected something transparent, or the
traditional triumph of order over chaos, were confounded. The
music was not only very progressive, but complex, puzzling and
provocative. Themes were introduced and interrupted, musical
quotations from his own and others' music were disguised and
quickly dismissed. Musically the tonal scheme seemed like a random
experiment (it eluded analysts for many years), the rhythm seemed
quirky, and the structure full of non sequiturs. Adding to the
contemporary listener's sense of frustration was the need for some
form of explanation.

The only known ciné footage of Carl Nielsen, taken in 1926, shows him in the home of his friend and patron C. J. Michaelsen.

Some of Nielsen's recent converts dismissed the symphony as a failure. Some loyal friends attributed it to angina, which causes depression; yet others reacted with anger. The critic Hugo Seligman was far-sighted when he described it as 'the work of the *youngest* of Danish composers, the boldest of them all'. Conservatives predictably dismissed its modern style – there was no dynamic or emerging tonality, nor was there evidence of a Schoenbergian twelve-note system, its structure was apparently disjointed, and its thematic material was briefly dismissed rather than developed. There was a clear contradiction in the complexity of the music and the simplicity of the title. Moreover, the composer's insistence on 'absolute music' seemed to contradict meanings which many listeners believe they can identify.

Nielsen's 'purely musical matters' *are* the work's extra-musical meaning
– the first movement is a statement on the currents of European
music. Music talking about music. And in the second movement
Nielsen is not defeated and unwell, but he portrays modern music as
such; this is a grotesque, but mercifully brief, parody.

The first riddle of Nielsen's final symphony is its intention of
simplicity, yet it was complexity that initially struck its first audience
(who saw it as an unsuccessful symphonic experiment from a master
of the genre). The second enigma is that the composer seems to have
concealed a programmatic content, while describing the work as
'absolute music'. And many consider it to be Nielsen's first pessimistic
symphony, in stark contrast to its predecessors.

Despite the composer's insistence that *Sinfonia semplice* contained
purely musical matters (the 'so-called absolute music'), by his juxta-
position of allusions to his own symphonies and the contrasting
musical styles of his rivals, the symphony is a statement on music itself
– although commenting humorously in the second movement, he
reaches a negative conclusion. The fourth movement is the most
thinly concealed autobiographical statement. Nielsen could only have
believed it to be 'so-called absolute music' if he considered his
reflections as merely templates for the musical construction. He had
so far only spoken or written of his own life with reticence, detachment, and often in the third person. By 1925 he felt sufficiently
distanced from his early years in Fyn to write about his childhood
after sustained persuasion by Irmelin. Now he spoke out musically
in what he must have felt was to be his last symphony: there is an
expression of personal suffering that is far more more characteristic in
the works of Gustav Mahler. Was this a reversal of Nielsen's optimistic
nature? Was Nielsen conscious of this or not? And was he misleading
himself – or us – by describing the symphony as concerning purely
musical matters?

The problem can be resolved by grasping Nielsen's central motto –
'Music is life' – so often quoted that it can bounce off our doors of
perception. Nielsen, despite his firm resolution against the Symbolist
trend of the fusion of the arts, wrote in 1920 to the editor Julius Rabe:

*I believe fully and firmly that the various arts can learn from one
another. That would not really be so strange, for when you look into the*

*elemental forces you find the same unbreakable law of order, development,
and coherence in all of them ... Naturally many false analogies can appear
as being apparently true ... Music is an art that either sleeps deeply ... or
exists more strongly than anything else. It is life or it is death. The other
arts* describe *life ... music* is *life ...*

Nielsen's final symphony deeply concerns the life of its composer
from a musical perspective. The English musicologist William Mann
wrote that 'All Mahler's symphonies are about different aspects of the
Life-force and the Death-force; this is a purview at once more definite
and circumscribed than that of any other symphonist ...' In this
statement he may possibly have overlooked Carl Nielsen, in whose
last symphony morbidity makes its first appearance. The composer
seems to have known that he had not much time to live, confiding to
Thorvald Nielsen that Variation IX in the Finale was 'death knocking
at the gate'. Having been given this clue Thorvald Nielsen began to
unravel the layers: 'It is not difficult to interpret what each instrument
represents: the big drum the knocking; the xylophone bony Death;
the deep tuba the black void. Nielsen explained, "But I want to defy
death – and then follows the flourish."'

Robert Simpson introduced a significant discovery in the second
edition of his book on Nielsen's symphonies. In the *Sinfonia semplice*
Nielsen had not, as Simpson had previously believed, abandoned the
use of evolving tonality, but had used it in a radical way which allowed
the work to find its own true nature. A key is targeted but expressed
by its prolonged *avoidance*. No wonder it was so hard to find! But how
better to express frustration and futility? Nielsen's first five symphonies
are about the *phenomenon* of life but the more soul-searching
Sixth Symphony is about the *meaning* of life. The music constantly
dissolves or disappears; it is arrested by barriers and reversals; it
expresses frustration and futility. Is that how everything seemed to
Nielsen in his last years? This is quite different to the youthful
optimism of his first three symphonies, but the powerful message of
the *Sinfonia semplice* invalidates the dismissal once made by Nielsen's
contemporaries that the Sixth was a miserable failure. Perhaps
the Sixth is not pessimistic but rather realistic and thus progressive.
After all, the musical quotations from his own works are perhaps
too brief or cryptic to be valedictory, and there is no trace of either

sentimentality or self pity. To a real world that is not always beautiful or hopeful Nielsen seeks an antidote rather than a heaven or
a paradise.

Had Nielsen composed by sketching and fleshing out, the *Sinfonia
semplice* might have turned out to be the diverting piece he envisaged
when he started work (even though a letter to Michaelsen had allowed
the possibility of stormy seas). In addition to the pause for inspiration
after the second movement, the symphony's gestation was extended
from August 1924 to December 1925 owing to commitments and
travels. Nielsen interrupted work on his symphony to compose the
music he had promised for the play *Ebbe Skammelsen* but a letter to
Marie indicated that the symphony was delayed for reasons of its own.
He was waiting 'to find the urge and the force from somewhere.
At the moment I feel much more inclined to take care of practical
matters. But I shall try again and keep trying until I find a way.'

He might well have said of his Sixth Symphony what Ralph
Vaughan Williams declared of his Fourth: 'I don't know whether I
like it, but it's what I meant.' Man remained at the centre of Nielsen's
art: he is ultimately resigned to life, the subject matter of all the
symphonies, but he is not depicted as being crushed. Nielsen's hero
will not accept defeat and will protest to the very end; in the words of
the Scottish conductor Bryden Thomson, 'The Sixth Symphony
ends with a valedictory raspberry.' Nielsen's final symphony would not
be published until 1937, six years after the composer's death, and
before the mid 1960s it was rarely performed.

In 1926 Nielsen spent some time in Florence with Søs. He bought a
second-hand Fiat in which he raced along Italy's dangerous mountain
roads. On the occasion of the twenty-fifth anniversary of Verdi's death
Nielsen attended a performance of Verdi's *Falstaff* conducted by
Toscanini in the little Rococo theatre in the mountain village of Buseto,
Verdi's birthplace. During the interval Nielsen and Toscanini met, and
the great conductor reassured Nielsen that he was familiar with the
Dane's music. Shortly after this Nielsen caught a fever, stopped work for
a while, and Marie came to join him. When he had recovered husband
and wife returned to Denmark, crossing the Alps in their Fiat; Marie
had to supervise the casting of her monument of Christian IX, now that
the great project was nearing its unveiling.

Holger Gilbert Jespersen, dedicatee and first performer of Nielsen's Flute Concerto; the work captures the flautist's fastidiously refined character

Through his illness Nielsen had lost time on the Flute Concerto which was due to be given a grand première in Paris on 21 October 1926 at the Salle Gaveau – part of a concert of works exclusively by Nielsen. Pages of the score were hastily sent in instalments to Gilbert Jespersen, its dedicatee, for rehearsal; and as the day of the concert approached, a provisional ending had to be used. Nielsen's supporters, who wished his music to reach more of an international audience, were delighted that a concert of his works was to be given in Paris. France was not the most receptive country to Scandinavian music, but some of the influential musicians who attended the concert of Nielsen's works were the composers Maurice Ravel and Albert Roussel. Arthur Honegger commended Nielsen: 'You formulated the aims for which we are all striving now, a generation before the rest of us.' The concert was sold out, and its atmosphere was vibrant.

*Opposite, a poster
advertising the first all-
Nielsen concert in France;
the programme included the
première of the Flute
Concerto, played by its
dedicatee Gilbert Jespersen.*

Nielsen, whose family had joined him for the event, described it as one of the greatest experiences of his life. His health, however, compelled him to delegate most of the conducting to Telmányi. The programme, in addition to the première of the Flute Concerto performed by its dedicatee, Gilbert Jespersen, comprised the Violin Concerto (with Peder Møller), the Fifth Symphony, five pieces from *Aladdin* and the Prelude to Act II of *Saul og David.* Nielsen was greatly impressed by the musicians of the Paris Conservatoire Orchestra who had started rehearsals uncommitted, but they had quickly warmed to Nielsen's music and to the Danish artists. At a lunch ceremony the following day he was appointed an Officer of the Légion d'Honneur.

When Gilbert Jespersen replaced Paul Hagemann in the Copenhagen Wind Quintet he inherited the promised flute concerto. It was not only Jespersen's fastidious character that was immortalized in the work, it was the refined character of the flute. From his days in the military band Nielsen was able to live and breathe music through wind instruments. 'The flute cannot belie its true nature, it comes from Arcadia and prefers the pastoral moods. Thus the composer is obliged to conform to its mild nature unless he would risk being branded as a barbarian.' He spoke of his developing method of composition early in the 1920s. 'I began composing with the piano which I later transposed for orchestra. The next stage was that I wrote my score directly for instruments. Now I think through the instruments themselves, almost as if I had crept into them. One can very well say that the instruments have a soul.'

In the Flute Concerto a trombone plays the role of a buffoon – quite unlike its menacing role in the Sixth Symphony – and it acts as a foil to the genteel flute, a dig at Jespersen. It has been suggested that the humorous trombone, an instrument Nielsen had played in the military band, may represent the composer, who said of this work that although the first movement begins with a dissonance, it is a dissonance of the 'gentler regions'. Nielsen continued, 'The beginning is, if anything, kept in a free, improvisatory style, and the solo instrument moves about as if seeking something, until it takes hold of a more decisive motive.' The second and final movement's original ending pursued a simple march-like theme that closed simply and happily in the key of D major. But between the première on 21 October and the

Bureau de Concerts : **Marcel de VALMALÈTE**, 45, rue La Boëtie, Paris (8ᵉ)
Téléphone : ELYSÉES 06-72

**Maison GAVEAU** (Salle des Concerts) | **JEUDI 21 OCTOBRE** 1926
45-47, rue **La Boëtie**, 45-47 | à **20 h. 45** (Ouverture des Portes, à **20 h. 15**)

## CONCERT SYMPHONIQUE

donné sous les auspices de l'ASSOCIATION FRANÇAISE d'EXPANSION et d'ÉCHANGES ARTISTIQUES
et consacré aux OEuvres de

# CARL NIELSEN

avec le concours de

## L'ORCHESTRE de la

### SOCIÉTÉ DES CONCERTS DU CONSERVATOIRE

sous la direction de **MM.**

## Carl NIELSEN et Emil TELMANYI

et MM.

## Peder MÖLLER et Holger Gilbert JESPERSEN
Violoniste        Flûtiste

1. Ouverture du 2ᵐᵉ acte de *Saül et David* (1902)
   sous la direction de **M. Emil Telmanyi**

2. *Concerto* pour violon et orchestre, op. 33 (1912)
   Soliste : **Poder Möller**
   sous la direction de **M. Emil Telmanyi**

3. *Symphonie nᵒ 5,* op. 50 (1920)
   sous la direction de **M. Emil Telmanyi**

4. *Concerto* pour flûte et orchestre (1926)
   Soliste : **M. Holger Gilbert Jespersen**

5. *Cinq morceaux tirés de l'* " *Aladdin* " (1919)
   a) Marche festivale d'Orient
   b) Le Rêve d'Aladdin et la Danse des brumes matinales
   c) Danse hindoue
   d) Le marché à Ispahan
   e) Danse nègre
   sous la direction de **l'Auteur**

**Places de 25 à 5 fr.** (*droits compris*). — En vente : **Maison Gaveau**; chez **Durand**, 4, pl. de la Madeleine; au **Guide-Billets**, 20, avenue de l'Opéra; chez **Rouart-Lerolle**, 40, boul. Malesherbes **Eschig**, 48, rue de Rome; **Senart**, 49, rue de Rome; **Roudanez, Laudy, Magasin Musical**, etc.

IMP. ALBERT PIGARD et JEAN ROBILLON réunies, 140, Faubourg Saint-Martin, Paris — 1926

next performance in Oslo on 9 November, Nielsen revised the concerto's ending, and created a far better joke. As a logical mirror of the
opening tonal meanderings the refined flute searches for the home
key at the end only to hear the vulgar trombone stumble onto it.

On 25 January 1927 Jespersen gave the concerto its Danish
première which received high praise from the Copenhagen critics,
who had largely chosen to pardon the Sixth Symphony as a temporary
aberration. Nielsen had described his first concerto for fifteen years
as mild, but in form and harmony – not to mention dramatic point –
it was an advance on his earlier concerto for violin. This humorous,
sparkling and vividly-coloured work, a favourite of the flautist's
repertoire, did not have any of the anguish of the Sixth Symphony.
It remained to be seen what would emerge in the concertos he had
undertaken to write for the other players of the Wind Quintet.

# IO

Nielsen c. 1927 with his
wife (right) and Irmelin's
mother-in-law, Mrs Frida
Møller (centre)

*Theories and prophesies are irrelevant. Some
believe in and hope for a new Messiah of art;
others think that all is in hopeless decline.
Both are unrealistic. The former believe in
miracles and want to witness them; the latter
that life may be extinguished to the last flicker.
They both forget that art is human and
that humanity will not die out in fifty or a
hundred years.*

Carl Nielsen, *Living Music,* 1925

## Final Statements 1927-31

From 1 January 1927 Nielsen was no longer conductor of the
Philharmonic Society; he had resigned the post on the advice of his
family. But the prestige he enjoyed enabled him still to do much to
influence and support Danish musical committees, organizations and
events. The celebrated Danish composer Vagn Holmboe (1909–96)
was one of many students who remembered Nielsen's encouragement
at this time. In 1927 entry to the Danish Conservatoire was considered
to be a matter of life and death. The violinist Anton Svenden had felt
that Holmboe might not be ready for the Conservatoire, but Nielsen
examined Holmboe's work and told him: 'You have been accepted.'
He would, however, advise others not to pursue musical careers,
always kindly but firmly.

In March, having been ordered to rest over the summer, Nielsen
yielded to the entreaties of his elder daughter and began to dictate his
childhood memories to her mother-in-law, Frida Møller. Irmelin had
often listened to her father's adventures and knew that they would
make a good book. But he had always shown a reluctance to discuss
himself and he worried that his stories would bore readers. The task
nevertheless began to absorb him and it was completed in six months.
*Min fynske barndom* ('My Childhood on Fyn') was published on
25 October 1927, two years after his collection of essays, *Living Music*.
It has since been translated into several languages, filmed, analysed by
literary critics and acclaimed as a vivid and witty portrait of a primitive rural upbringing.

The day was fast approaching when Marie's mighty statue of the
late King Christian IX was to be unveiled. The culmination of fifteen
years' work, it was now more of a monument to its creator than to
its subject. Often her family had begged her to abandon the project,
since by the end of World War I the money available to her had been
reduced in value by inflation so she had had to pay for some studies
and castings herself. 'Once I worked out a list of all the delays and
postponements,' she told a newspaper two days before the unveiling

Anne Marie Carl-Nielsen's equestrian monument of King Christian IX leaves the brass founders in November 1927. 'Even if you modelled like an angel,' the sculptress had been advised in1906, 'a woman would never be given such a task.'

ceremony on 15 November 1927. 'It was a long one. Maybe you won't believe this, but the strangest thing is that I'm a pretty fast worker. Of my fifteen years' work there were thirteen years of delays.' During that time she had worked on planks twenty feet off the ground without ever falling but on one occasion a lump of plaster had fallen on her and she was rushed to hospital to receive stitches. The worst moment of all? 'When it was completely finished, it disintegrated during the casting.' Marie had started from the beginning again, but this time increasing the scale by twenty-five per cent! All arguments with the committee were forgotten on the day of the ceremony itself. Speeches followed a military procession, and the Royal Family thanked the famous artistic couple – Anne Marie in her fur coat, Carl in his top hat – for all that they had achieved in their respective fields. The king publicly thanked the artist, craftsmen and the fundraising committee for their work in raising a statue to their former monarch. Other members of the Royal Family made flattering comments to the distinguished artistic couple regarding their contribution to Danish culture. The king specifically congratulated Nielsen on his recent success in Leipzig, referring to the Fifth Symphony's performance under Furtwängler on 27 October 1927. The symphony had created waves in Germany three months previously at the International Festival of Contemporary Music in Frankfurt, despite criticism of Furtwängler's performance (Nielsen was disappointed by the conductor's choice of slow tempos).

The Danish Radio Symphony Orchestra had been established two years previously, and in 1927 Nielsen was invited to conduct the first orchestral broadcast on Danish Radio. Even though he accepted the invitation, he despaired of music's emaciation across the wireless and denounced the 'crackling gramophone'. In this year he maintained his hectic schedule, serving as a member of the jury of the International Schubert Competition, and conducting a series of concerts in Stockholm. Some of his family joined him in Amsterdam when the French conductor Pierre Monteux, on 15 December, performed the Fifth Symphony with the Concertgebouw Orchestra and the Violin Concerto with Telmányi as soloist. According to Søs, her father found the interpretation too refined and Gallic. 'The concert,' she wrote, 'was quite an occasion, but all the time Father sat with a rather disappointed look in his eyes.'

One orchestral piece was composed in this year – *En fantasirejse til Færøerne* ('An Imaginary Journey to the Faroe Islands'), a 'rhapsody overture'. It was commissioned for two concerts at which fifty inhabitants of the Faroe Islands were invited to perform national songs at Copenhagen's Theatre Royal. Nielsen agreed to give the work's première on 27 November, and as often happened, he left things too late and was struggling to meet the deadline. The visit, however, was cancelled due to a flu epidemic. Then the performers' ship was delayed a few days by an Atlantic hurricane: the overture had prophetically depicted a sea voyage and storm. The performance did not take place until January 1928. *En fantasirejse til Færøerne* was followed by the strains of the Faroese hymn *Easter Bells Chimed Softly*, which gave way to a dancing song. Nielsen dismissed his overture as 'nothing more than a piece of jobbery', but it has become a popular concert piece. He was surprised to read in several newspapers the day after its performance that he had written a work 'with striking similarities to Sibelius' – whom he would meet the following year at the Scandinavian Music Festival in Copenhagen. Embarrassed by the obvious imbalance of their worldly success, Sibelius most generously told Nielsen, 'I don't even reach your ankles.'

In December that year the violinist Fini Henriques celebrated his sixtieth birthday, and among the greetings to him published by *Politiken* Nielsen contributed eight bars of music. Emil Telmányi implored his father-in-law to turn them into a full composition for violin solo; thus it became the *Prelude and Presto* dedicated to Henriques but first performed by Telmányi on 14 April 1928 at a concert of new music at Borup's High School. It received high praise from audience and critics: 'A sparkling work, full of humour, wit and technical violin wonder,' according to Hugo Seligman; the critic Kai Flor wrote of its '... charm and fantasy, light and power – something of the same musical enchantment and purity as a Bachian chaconne'.

The years from 1925 to 1927 had exposed Nielsen to the different directions of modern music, and he carefully evaluated the new techniques and sonorities before deciding which of them to absorb into his own compositions. In the Three Piano Pieces of 1927, Nielsen exploited new musical techniques that he had largely bypassed before then. These keyboard pieces are not parodies (as in the *Humoresque* of the Sixth Symphony) but they are highly concentrated essays in the manner of Arnold Schoenberg's Second Viennese School. Tonality disintegrates, they are full of impressionistic effects, and, particularly in the fugue of the third piece, they exploit Schoenberg's newly developed twelve-note composition (all twelve notes of the chromatic scale are ordered into a set that is then subject to repetition, inversion, retrograde and other transpositions). The medieval *diabolus in musica*, the interval of the augmented fourth, appropriately puts in an appearance, and a bass drum effect is achieved by the striking of a handful of bass notes. While the pieces bear Nielsen's fingerprints they in reality form his response to the European avant garde rather than following his individual path into the twentieth century. But the Three Piano Pieces may represent a foreshadowing of a later symphonic style, had Nielsen tackled a seventh symphony.

The modern idiom introduced in Nielsen's next woodwind concerto was in contrast to the milder nature of the Flute Concerto, the first of the promised set of five. Early in 1928, Nielsen's friend and patron, Carl Johan Michaelsen, prompted him to begin the clarinet

'I don't even reach your ankles': Jean Sibelius to Carl Nielsen. Sibelius (far left) and Wilhelm Stenhammar (front) are photographed with Nielsen at the Festival of Scandinavian Music, Copenhagen, 1926.

concerto for Aage Oxenvad. Work on it started during a skiing holiday in Norway with his wife, where he broke two ribs despite doctor's orders to take things easy. 'If I must live like an invalid then I have no desire to live,' he replied. Marie went on to Carrara in Italy to do some carving and when her husband felt well enough, he travelled alone to Damgaard where he could work without interruptions. He was well aware that this new work was different. To Nancy Dalberg he wrote: 'I actually have no idea how it will sound. Maybe it won't sound good, but I will not compose music if I always have to compose in the same manner.' Describing his new technique, he said that he was thinking through the instrument and found the clarinet to be something wild and troll-like. On another occasion he said it could be 'at once warm-hearted, and completely hysterical, gentle as balm and screaming as a streetcar on poorly lubricated rails'. From Damgaard he began to send instalments for Oxenvad with letters to Søs and Telmányi and, as before, he enjoyed his escape from Copenhagen. 'Even the temptation to slip over and visit you or call you on the telephone has now died. Here all unrest is soothed in the sighing of the trees outside my window. Strange how everything changes! We are as motes of dust and nothing amid time and space; in freedom and peace there is actually the greatest life.'

The Clarinet Concerto was first performed by Oxenvad and twenty-two musicians in the drawing room of Michaelsen's summer house on 14 September 1928. Telmányi conducted. Afterwards there was polite discussion of the work and it was considered to be good, despite being quite unlike its counterpart for flute. Telmányi aptly dubbed the concerto, which was written as one continuous movement, as 'music from another planet'. Orchestral sonorities are dark and sparse, and the snare drum is a prominent feature. Aware of the difficulties, Nielsen reassured Michaelsen: 'Every bar has been thought out, turned inside out, and examined, in order to make it as clear and malleable as possible. In that respect one can naturally say that it represents a very fine effort on the part of the composer ... But if Oxenvad can make nothing of it there is no one who can.'

The first public performance was on 11 October in Copenhagen; here it was not well received. Its Swedish première in Stockholm was its next performance, after which it was denounced by Olaf Petersen-Berger as 'absolutely the worst thing that this slightly too obviously

experimental and provocatively sidestepping Dane has yet put
together ... Nielsen hereby confesses himself to be a cacophonist. Not
knowing any better he seeks to keep up with the times.' Oxenvad
was quoted as saying that Nielsen must have known how to play the
clarinet himself, as he could not otherwise have found the very hardest
notes to play. 'All the papers are cool towards the concerto,' Nielsen
complained to Telmányi, but on 10 December it was performed again
in Copenhagen with results that rewarded Oxenvad's efforts. Greater
triumph came in Göteborg on 7 April the following year, and this
Nielsen attributed to the good relations he enjoyed with the orchestra.
Their enthusiasm for the concerto revealed the modern masterpiece
that it is: bleak, raw, arguably lacking in seductive calm or beauty (it
is – as Telmányi described it – like the strange landscape of an alien
planet), its depth and intensity, together with its stylistic fusion of
progressive techniques within Classical structures, make it – along
with the later symphonies – one of Nielsen's great works. It was to
influence future compositions by Nielsen, notably *Amor og digteren*
('Cupid and the Poet') of 1930.

On 1 November 1928 the recently-founded Danish State Radio
Symphony Orchestra conducted by Jarosław Krupka broadcast the
Bohemian-Danish Folk Tune, which Nielsen had written for a special
concert of Czech music. This piece for string orchestra was based
on both a Czech song and a traditional Danish song about Queen
Dagmar, the Bohemian princess married to King Valdemar Sejr
(1170–1241). It is a charming piece which might well have followed his
*Little Suite for Strings* of forty years before, rather than the tough-fibred
Clarinet Concerto or the Three Piano Pieces from the same year.

On 25 November Nielsen, against the wishes of a heart-specialist in
Copenhagen, left the city for Göteborg, this time to rehearse a work
he had not heard for many years. *Saul og David* was to be given at
Göteborg's Great Theatre. Once again the city rose to the challenge.
Nielsen sent the details in a long letter to Telmányi, in which he
praised the young Norwegian conductor, a Mr Kjelland, for getting
the tempos quite correct. Although he found the orchestra of forty-six
players to have been a little harsh in sound, he felt that the whole
production had life and movement. Nielsen in this performance was
one of the first to hear Kirsten Flagstad, a young Norwegian soprano
who went on to achieve international acclaim; in the role of Michal

The Norwegian soprano
Kirsten Flagstad; in the role
of Michal she contributed
greatly to the success of the
1928 production of *Saul
og David*.

she was 'simply first class in both singing and acting'. The opera
played to full houses, running for fifteen performances, and the
production was highly praised by the Swedish and Danish critics.
Nielsen was so delighted that he summoned Irmelin – and when
Marie also joined him, Mannheimer booked the couple into the
best room in Stockholm's Grand Hotel.

While in Sweden Nielsen conducted a concert of his own music –
it was well received except for the Clarinet Concerto – then he gave a
radio concert (still a novelty to him). At a time when *Saul og David*
was not even in the repertoire of Copenhagen's Theatre Royal – a
sore point with Nielsen – the Swedes had taken the opera to heart,
broadcasting it from Stockholm on 16 September 1931 (with a
different cast that included Jussi Björling in the role of Jonathan).

Nielsen was becoming aware of his unsustainable pace, as both
mental and physical exhaustion beset him for longer periods. From
Göteborg he wrote: 'Travel, work, duties, worry and travel again –
these govern my whole existence. Music is certainly an art that
interferes, demands and lives; so that all the time one must dance
attendance or she will die ... Do you know what I have done since 26th
November?' An impressive list followed. As Thorvald Nielsen, pointed
out: 'The mental energy manifested by the great works of his last years
forms an unaccountable contrast to his increasing bodily debilitation.'

The final three years of Nielsen's life were distinguished by a fresh challenge he set himself: to write music which combined the plain art of ancient polyphony with modern tonal sonorities. To this end, he resumed his studies of Palestrina and the old Dutch masters. The most important results of his endeavour were first the Three Motets for unaccompanied choir, set to three Psalms of King David, and then *Commotio* for organ, regarded by many of its admirers as Nielsen's most remarkable achievement. These works were not written as a result of any late religious awakening: Nielsen, though not a believer himself, had always been sympathetic in his approach to sacred matters. After his sixty-fifth birthday he wrote to Thorvald Aagaard: 'It's perfectly natural that time passes and goes on passing, and when the time comes that I can no longer work, I believe the Wholeness will take all my thoughts and work. In that sense I shan't die. That's true compassion. It's nothing to do with grace to the individual, just that in the end it cannot be otherwise.'

Apart from an attempt at a Fantasia for Organ in 1913 Nielsen had only written one minor prelude for the instrument, around the turn of the century. In early 1929, as part of his studies of polyphony, he wrote twenty-eight preludes at the request of Johannes Hansen, the head teacher at Rødovre. Hansen objected to their lack of solemnity and felt that they were unsuitable for use in church. Nielsen agreed with this criticism, but told Hansen that he believed attitudes would change. All but one, however, were performed at a concert in Skovshoved Church on 1 January 1930 by Poul Schierbeck. Schierbeck had refused to play No. 26 in a church, but although this prelude is indeed lacking in solemnity, it hardly merits righteous indignation.

The première of the complete set was given by Peter Thomsen in Copenhagen's Church of St. Johannes on 19 March 1930; the collection was published later that year. Rather than exhibiting the characteristics of Nielsen's songs, chamber or symphonic works, the organ preludes are true to their own genre, arising directly from the world of the great Baroque organists and composers, Girolamo Frescobaldi, Samuel Scheidt and Johan Pachelbel. They are a remarkable product of a composer who must have gained enjoyment from writing successfully in such widely differing types of music.

In 1928 Nielsen had been appreciative of a concert given by the Palestrina Choir directed by the distinguished Danish musician,

Mogens Wöldike. Of the old Dutch motets, *Vox in Rama* by Clemens most impressed Nielsen, and Wöldike was quick to suggest that the composer should write something for his choir. Eventually Nielsen, together with help from his wife, who both understood and inspired him, found some of the Psalms of King David and, as with *Hymnus amoris*, had them translated into Latin. He became highly absorbed in this work, the Three Motets, Op. 55, and finished it at Silkeborg Spa, where Carl and Marie took a cure together in 1929. In the motets, especially *Afflictus sum*, he expressed an almost superhuman grief and despair: 'I am cold as death, I pray from my heart's unrest.' *Dominus regit me* ('The Lord is my Shepherd') and *Benedictus Dominus* ('Praise the Lord') are both beautiful settings and in their purity of style resemble the great choral masters of the sixteenth century.

The process of composition over the summer was extremely con-centrated – like the music itself. 'I am taking great care, and am so occupied with it that every note is an event,' Nielsen wrote to Marie in June 1929. '... my symphonic talent and familiarity with the larger instrumental forms (sonatas, symphonies, etc.) are not the slightest use in this context and I must even suppress ideas leading in many different directions in order to rise to a higher altitude and approach

Mogens Wöldike, conductor of Copenhagen's Palestrina Choir; a concert by the choir was the inspiration for Nielsen's Three Motets.

the old masters who hover there, pure and great like arch angels on the border of heaven. I do not imitate them, but I model myself upon them.' The first performance of the motets was given on 11 April 1930 by the dedicatees in Copenhagen's Glyptotek Museum (where Nielsen had first heard the choir). Expectations and excitement ran high, and it was generally agreed that Nielsen had contributed something of great importance in a genre which was entirely new to him.

Defying doctors' orders once again, Nielsen conducted two more concerts in Göteborg. On 12 August he participated in the 125th anniversary of the birth of Hans Christian Andersen which was celebrated in summer in Odense. There he performed dramatic music that he had recently written for soloists, choir and orchestra to a short one-act play by S. Michaelis, *Amor og digteren* ('Cupid and the Poet'). The play combined the theme of Andersen's fairytale, *The Naughty Boy*, with his autobiographical account of his meeting with the opera singer, Jenny Lind, 'the Swedish Nightingale', on Christmas Eve, Berlin, in 1845. Its short orchestral overture is recognizably in Nielsen's mature style, especially that of the Clarinet Concerto: modern, rhythmically angular, not lyrical as arguably befits the historical themes. Both the overture and the concerto score the clarinet and snare drum in dialogue, a rare instance of Nielsen repeating an innovation. The songs in the work are however very fresh. *The Italian Shepherd's Song* is an elegant pastiche, and *We Love You, Our Lofty North* is a bravura number worthy of a diva like Jenny Lind.

On a misty evening in October 1930 Copenhagen inflicted another blow on Nielsen when he was knocked down by a tram-car, and thrown about eighteen feet into the street. He was taken to the Municipal Hospital and found to be slightly concussed, with a dislocated shoulder and collar bone. The family worried about the inevitable strain caused to his heart but within a month he was at work again. His studies in ancient polyphony had suggested to him that a quest for musical universality, free of any period or subjectivity, might best be expressed by music for the organ. Two further preludes were composed before he set out on his masterpiece for this instrument, *Commotio.*

Nielsen felt that none of his earlier works demanded such great concentration from him as this one. In the work he was trying to re-establish, as he put it, 'the only really valid organ style, namely the

*Opposite*, Nielsen with laurels, Göteborg, December 1930. Sweden was arguably ahead of Denmark in recognizing Nielsen's achievements.

polyphonic music that is especially suited to this instrument; it has for
a long time been regarded as a kind of orchestra, which it *certainly is
not.*' On 2 March 1931 he wrote to his wife: 'Now my big piece for
organ is quite ready and I am pleased with the work, for it has been
created with greater skill than all of my other things ... It's a long work
and lasts about twenty-two minutes. Bach's largest organ work (the
Prelude and Fugue in E minor) lasts for 368 bars, mine is 511, and so
with regard to length ...? But Bach is unequalled ... '

On 24 April Peter Thomsen played *Commotio* to the composer and
a circle of his friends on the organ to which Nielsen had had access
during composition (in the Palace Chapel at Christianborg). Among
those present was Emilius Bangert who gave its première at Aarhus
Cathedral on 14 August 1931. Nielsen disagreed with the soloist's
suggested revisions but did make some changes. Bangert planned
to give a recital on 6 October as part of Lübeck's German–Nordic
Festival, which Nielsen would not be able to attend, but he wrote a
programme note for this performance: 'The Latin word *Commotio* (to
be moved to feeling) actually applies to all music, but the word has a
special usage here as an expression for self-objectivization. In a major
work for the mighty instrument we call the organ, whose notes are
produced by the natural element we call air, the composer must try to
suppress all personal, lyrical feelings.' As an esoteric work that bal-
anced traditional restraints with modern musical techniques, it was
met with mixed feelings which continue to deny it the audience – and
the attention – deserved by a truly remarkable masterpiece. *Commotio*
is like a monument, impressive, but monolithic and forbidding. It
commands attention. A listener's fascination grows with each hearing
as the timeless piece begins to communicate its secrets. It does not
change nor does it move, yet it has life and energy.

In January 1931 Nielsen was honoured by being appointed director
of the Copenhagen Conservatoire but he liked neither the formalities
which went with the position nor the awe in which the young
students held his high office. Søs became alarmed by how quickly her
father's hair was turning white and how suddenly his always boyish
face had aged over the previous summer. When Nielsen visited
Irmelin in north Sjælland, and she noted her father's depression and
his regret that unless he himself or another Danish artist took the
initiative, his works were still only rarely performed outside

Scandinavia. 'I know I've done my work as well as possible,' he complained, 'but I wonder if it is to any effect.'

The education of the next Danish musical generation was close to Nielsen's heart, and several of his compositions from this period are didactic. *Klavermusik for smaa og store* ('Piano Music for Young and Old', literally 'Small and Great') was written in response to a commission from the Danish Music Teachers Association. Nielsen aimed to write twenty-four pieces, proceeding up and down through the circle of fifths in the first and second volumes respectively. Twenty-five enchanting little pieces emerged (two of them in G major), all within a five-finger range. In December 1929 Nielsen had delivered a lecture to the Danish Music Teaching Society, and in response to its request for something folk-like and simple in character he wrote Allegretto for Two Recorders. He also wrote six rounds (vocal canons) the following year 'for use in Schools and Training Colleges'.

Although his family, for his health's sake, begged him to go to a resort after the summer, Nielsen returned to Copenhagen for the start of the musical season. He was excited by the première of *Commotio* and delighted by a revival of *Maskarade* which he wanted to supervise. The production at the Theatre Royal was under the baton of the talented Italian conductor, Egisto Tango. But late in September, caught up in the excitement of the rehearsals, Nielsen over-exerted himself. His heart became weaker, and in great pain, he finally heeded medical advice. On 1 October he listened on hospital earphones to the Danish Radio broadcast of his Violin Concerto, a performance he had hoped to conduct. A blood clot was found near his heart. On the evening of 2 October he lost consciousness at the point in *Maskarade* when Corporal Mors came on stage at the Theatre Royal, and as Emilius Bangert was rehearsing *Commotio* on the organ of St Mary's at Lübeck prior to his recital.

Late at night on 3 October Nielsen briefly regained consciousness. He saw his family gathered at his bedside. 'You're all standing as though you're in a waiting room. You are waiting.'

On his death a feeling of desolation swept throughout the Scandinavian countries where he had so many friends and admirers. It seemed impossible that a flame of such vitality could be extinguished, that so much music from him would now never be written.

Carl Nielsen's funeral,
9 October, in Copenhagen
Cathedral. The death of
such a respected figure
had an emotional impact
throughout Denmark.

On 9 October at 2 o'clock in the Free Church in Copenhagen the family assembled once again. A laurel wreath from the King and Queen of Denmark dominated hundreds which lay along the entire length of the cathedral. Tributes were received from the many distinguished Orders to which the man of humble birth had been elected: the Order of the Dannebrog from his own nation, the Academies of Art in both Sweden and Germany, the Légion d'Honneur of France, Sweden's Order of the Pole Star, the Knights of the Crown Order of Italy, the Icelandic Order of the Falcon, and the Norwegian Order of St. Olav.

Anne Marie's last image of Carl, a marble bust for the Göteborg Concert Hall

Many of Nielsen's colleagues paid their respects that day by performing his music: Mogens Wöldike played one of Nielsen's Preludes; a chamber orchestra conducted by Telmányi performed the Andante Lamentoso which had been written to commemorate Oluf Hartmann's death; the hymn *My Jesus Make my heart to love Thee* was played to Nielsen's melody; the Palestrina Choir sang the psalm *Dominus regit me* in the setting Nielsen had recently written for them; and to conclude the cathedral service, Egisto Tango conducted the Andante from Nielsen's Third Symphony, *Sinfonia espansiva*. At the graveside the Copenhagen Wind Quintet played the chorale and variations from the Wind Quintet; finally, at the graveside, the Students' Choral Society sang Nielsen's song *Aftenstemning* ('Evening Mood').

The funeral was a state ritual that befitted Denmark's greatest composer of the twentieth century, but it was also a very personal occasion. Many mourners broke down with grief at the loss of their friend. In the inner ear of one, Nielsen's words might have re-echoed:

*I dismiss the idea of an eternal life, and don't know if I want to live forever. I do not believe in supernatural things. Many things that look like miracles to us are natural phenomena governed by laws we have failed to comprehend.*

Music is life: in life it had represented Nielsen's observation of the unity and diversity behind every living thing. Now music was his immortality.

Many monuments to the composer were suggested soon after his death. Two were completed, both by his widow, Anne Marie, and

The Herd Boy playing a
Wooden Flute, one of two
monuments to Nielsen
sculpted by his widow, was
unveiled on 9 June 1933
at Nielsen's birthplace.

both demonstrate her personal and artistic empathy with her
late husband. The first and more modest work, *The Herd Boy
playing a Wooden Flute*, may be seen at the composer's birthplace at
Nørre Lyndelse. It was unveiled at a ceremony on 9 June 1933, on
what would have been Nielsen's sixty-eighth birthday.

The more ambitious monument, *The Young Man playing Pan-
pipes on a Wingless Pegasus*, is situated in Copenhagen at the road
junction at Grønningen near Østerport, and was unveiled there on
17 December 1939. Anne Marie Carl-Nielsen explained: 'What I
wanted to show in my figure is the forward movement, the sense of
life, the fact that nothing stands still. I wanted to create a plastic
expression of what Carl called "Living Music". I want my horse to
evoke a sense of weather: sun, wind and showers, for the very reason
that there's so much weather in Carl Nielsen's music, and such big,
strange birds.'

To find the composer's real monument, however, we must use our ears not our eyes. We must listen to his music and to that which followed him. 'Whenever a new Danish work is introduced,' said the Danish composer Knudåge Riisager, 'it will invariably be judged on the dual criterion: *out of,* or *not out of* Carl Nielsen.'

# Epilogue

While it is generally agreed that Carl Nielsen is the central figure of twentieth-century Danish music, describing either his achievement or his influence brings forth a multiplicity of response. He has been, for convenience, labelled anti-Romantic: but this unhelpful and inaccurate label suggests that he brought one type of Danish music to an end. Nielsen was a rugged and practical individualist, not one inclined to conform to contemporary vogues and expectations. He did not specialize, but wrote in a bewildering and expanding aesthetic. Unity is to be found in the representation of the patterns and forces underlying everything that lives, breathes and utters sound, especially from the humanistic perspective of man at the central role – observer and observed.

His Conservatoire studies he cut to the minimum, absorbing only what he considered would be of direct use to him. Although he had composed since his youth, he did not include composition in his Conservatoire curriculum. He only briefly wrote in the style of Brahms and Svendsen. As his powers in composition increased so his music became more individual and therefore less likely to establish any Nielsen school. His path towards twentieth-century sonorities was independent from any group of like-minded or local composers. This presented the next generation of Danish composers with a dilemma.

In Denmark Nielsen's songs are certainly celebrated, although while people sing them, they are not necessarily aware of who wrote them. Outside Denmark, it is, of course, the symphonies which have placed him in the front rank of European composers, although his admirers confidently wait for the embers of his keyboard, chamber, choral and operatic music to ignite into flames of popularity. In his own country Nielsen's music is proudly performed and anniversaries respected but compared to the investment by other nations in their major composers, Denmark could have done more.

A nine-year project headed by Niels Martin Jensen began as late as 1994 on the first comprehensive and scholarly publication of Nielsen's musical scores. Only the piano works have been published after thorough research and corrections. By 1994 none of the stage works had even been printed; the Fifth Symphony, acknowledged as a twentieth-century masterpiece, existed in what almost amounted to a flawed private edition until republished in 1950, edited by the conductor Erik Tuxen. (Emil Telmányi was credited as joint editor, but criticized Tuxen for going beyond correction and restoration.) Orchestras throughout the world are therefore confused between two equally inadequate scores. The Carl Nielsen Archive only issued its catalogue of musical manuscripts to scholars and musicians in 1992, completing a task begun in 1935. And the continuing embargo on the literary manuscripts not yet catalogued hampers research.

Arguably Carl Nielsen's individuality closed his own school. Some Danes even argued that his influence was negative, for two identifiable groups of reasons. The progressives said that the next generation of Danish composers rejected European trends because of Nielsen's conservative views – that Stravinsky's music was threadbare, Schoenberg's dissonant, Bartók's 'modern'. (Another explanation for the eclipse of foreign music was the German occupation of Denmark in 1940. The Danish Lieder singer, Aksel Schiøtz, became a national rallying symbol and thousands of Danes flocked to his leading of community singing where patriotic and popular songs – including those by Nielsen – dominated the programme.)

But the second group of reactionaries against Nielsen felt great resentment that he had single-handedly destroyed the Golden Age of Danish Romanticism. Outspoken in this view was another Danish individualist, Rued Langgaard (1893–1952), a hyper-Romantic and religious mystic whose career was totally eclipsed by Nielsen. Langgaard's dispute with his domestic rival was bitter, and in his oratorio the phrase *Carl Nielsen vor store komponist* ('Carl Nielsen, Our Great Composer') is repeated continuously, leaving the listener in no doubt of his sarcasm. On Nielsen's death Langgaard told a newspaper: 'The importance of Carl Nielsen is to have torn down what Niels W. Gade built up. I have nothing to add.'

How can an objective conclusion on Nielsen's achievement be reached given such polarized opinions? Was it 'progressive tonality'? Or his organic methods, or his fluidity of rhythm (his so-called 'current')? Across the broad spectrum, from his high art to his popular songs, the only common thread to be found is its individuality, and the central focus of the phenomenon of Man. His music spans from the most earthy to the most sublime extremes; of the latter his final symphony contains the most ingenious, clear but cryptic, autobiographical statements of a composer who clearly understood that only music can express such extremes. This understanding was both the incentive and the reward of his life's work.

He was a man of the soil who formed a spontaneous view of the spiritual world and his music reflected what he observed rather than what people might be speculating. Writing in 1907, he said, 'I wonder if there will ever come a time one day when we will all gather together in peace and quiet and talk of all these things that please us most and bind us together, all of us who have a common cause. Yes, the older I grow, the more I can understand the craving for a thoroughly spiritual relationship between like-minded people. It has haunted the mind of mankind long before Socrates and Christ. It will forever shadow their dreams. Unfortunately I do not believe in such a possibility after death, so it's all the more sad that one cannot draw all those friends together in a circle during life.'

I leave it to Oscar Geismar, who gave the eulogy at Nielsen's funeral service, to offer the final word on Carl Nielsen the man and artist:

*An artist can be a seeker after truth who can express the inexpressible. In this noble sense Carl Nielsen was an artist ... He believed in the Spirit of Nature. He was the son of Niels the Painter from Nørre Lyndelse and he would be no one else.*

# Classified List of Works

The full catalogue of Carl Nielsen's musical and literary œuvre published in 1965 established many dates and details that had previously been uncertain, and discovered a few lost manuscripts and works. Nielsen had no time for proof-reading, and was not always conscientious about keeping a record of which piece had been sent to which printers. Many of his works have no opus number, and some opus numbers are not attached to works. Nielsen's compositions are therefore properly identified by the FS item number from the 1965 catalogue by Dan Fog and Torben Schousboe. This list presents Nielsen's principal musical compositions, grouped by genre.

The abbreviation 'fp' denotes first public performance, where known; dates of recitals to private subscribers are included, but those of private gatherings by invitation are not – the exception being *Ved en ung kunstners baare* ('At the Bier of a Young Artist'), written for the funeral of the painter Oluf Hartmann. Unless otherwise stated, the city in which works were first performed was Copenhagen. After the composition date, the list gives details of excerpts (songs, orchestral suites, etc.) from dramatic productions which were published separately.

## Stage Works

### Operas

*Saul og David* ('Saul and David'), FS25, opera in four acts to a libretto by E. Christiansen after the First and Second Books of Samuel (1898–1901).
fp 28 November 1902

*Maskarade* ('Masquerade'), FS39, comic opera in three acts to a libretto by V. Andersen, after the play by Holberg (1904–6). fp 11 November 1906

## Music for Theatre/Musicals

*En aften paa Giske* ('An Evening on Giske'), FS9, text by A. Munch (1889). fp 15 January 1890

*Snefrid*, FS17, text by H. Drachmann (1893).
fp 10 April 1894

*Atalanta*, FS30, text by G. Wied (1901).
fp 19 December 1901

*Hr. Oluf han rider* ('Sir Oluf Rides'), FS37, text by H. Drachmann (1906) [three songs and Elves Dance].
fp 9 October 1906

*Tove*, FS43, text by L. Holstein (1906–8) [four songs].
fp 20 March 1908

*Willemoes*, FS44, text by L. C. Nielsen (1907–8) [five songs]. fp 7 February 1908

*Forældre* ('The Parents'), FS45, text by O. Bentzon (1908). fp 9 February 1908

*Ulvens søn* ('The Wolf's Son'), FS50, text by J. Aakjær (1909) [two songs]. fp Aarhus, 14 November 1909

*Hagbarth og Signe* ('Hagbarth and Signe'), FS57, text by A. Oehlenschlæger (1910) [one song, one dance].
fp 4 June 1910

*Sankt Hansaftenspil*, ('Midsummer Night's Play'), FS65, text by A. Oehlenschlæger (1913). fp 3 June 1913

*Fæderland* ('The Fatherland'), FS71, text by E. Christiansen (1915) [one march, one song].
fp 5 February 1916

Prologue to the Shakespeare Celebrations, FS80, text by H. Rode (1916) [Ariel's song]. fp Elsinore, 24 June 1916

*Løgneren* ('The Liar'), FS88. Text by J. Sigurjónsson (1918) [one song]. fp 15 February 1918

*Aladdin*, Op. 34, FS89, text by A. Oehlenschlæger (1918–19) [three songs, suite for orchestra]. fp 15 and 22 February 1919

*Moderen* ('The Mother[land]'), Op. 41, FS94, text by H. Rode (1920). fp 30 January 1921

*Cosmus*, FS98, text by E. Christiansen (1921–2). fp 25 February 1922

*Ebbe Skammelsen*, FS117, text by H. Bergstedt (1925). fp 25 June 1925

*Amor og digteren* ('Love and the Poet'), Op. 54, text by S. Michaelis, FS150 (1930) [two songs and overture]. fp Odense, 12 August 1930

*Paaske-aften* ('Easter-eve'), FS156, text by N. F. S. Grundtvig (1931). fp 4 April 1931

**Orchestral**

*Symphonic Rhapsody* in F, FS7 (1888). fp 24 February 1893

Symphony No. 1 in G minor, Op. 7, FS16 (1890–92). fp 14 March 1894

Symphony No. 2, *De fire temperamenter* ('The Four Temperaments'), Op. 16, FS29 (1901–2). fp 1 December 1902

Symphony No. 3, *Sinfonia espansiva*, Op. 27, FS60 (1910–11). fp 28 February 1912

Symphony No. 4, *Det uudslukkelige* ('The Inextinguishable'), Op. 29, FS76 (1914–16). fp 1 February 1916

Symphony No. 5, Op. 50, FS97 (1921–2). fp 24 January 1922

Symphony No. 6, *Sinfonia semplice* ('Simple Symphony'), FS116 (1924–5). fp 11 December 1925

Violin Concerto, Op. 33, FS61 (1911). fp 28 February 1912

Flute Concerto, FS119 (1926). fp Paris, 21 October 1926

Clarinet Concerto, Op. 57, FS129 (1928). fp 11 October 1928

*Little Suite for Strings*, Op. 1, FS6 (1888). fp 8 September 1888

*Helios*, overture, Op. 17, FS32 (1903). fp 8 October 1903

*Saga-drøm*, overture, Op. 39, FS46 (1907–8). fp 6 April 1908

*Nærmere Gud til dig* ('Nearer my God to Thee'), paraphrase for wind instruments, FS63 (1912). fp 22 August 1915

*Pan og Syrinx* ('Pan and Syrinx'), Op. 49, FS87 (1917–18). fp 11 February 1918

*En Fantasirejse til Færøerne* ('An Imaginary Trip to the Faroe Islands'), rhapsodic overture, FS123 (1927), fp 27 November 1927

*Bøhemisk–dansk folktone* ('Bohemian–Danish Folktune'), paraphrase for string orchestra, FS130 (1928). fp 1 November 1928

**Choral**

*Hymnus amoris*, Op. 12, FS21, text by A. Olrik, Latin translation by J. L. Heiberg (1896–7). fp 27 April 1897

Cantata for the Lorens Frølich Festival, FS26, text by A. Olrik (1900). fp 30 November 1900

Cantata for the Students' Association, FS31, text by H. Drachmann (1901). fp 1 January 1901

*Søvnen* ('The Sleep'), Op. 18, FS33, text by J. Jørgensen (1903–4). fp 21 March 1905

Cantata for the Anniversary of Copenhagen University,
Op. 24, FS47, text by N. Møller (1908).
fp 29 October 1908

Cantata for the Commemoration of 11 February 1659,
for the 250th anniversary of the storming of
Copenhagen, FS49, text by L. C. Nielsen (1909).
fp 11 February 1909

Cantata for the National Exhibition at Aarhus, FS54,
text by L. C. Nielsen; collaboration with E. Bangert
(1909). fp Aarhus, 18 May 1909

Cantata for the Commemoration of P. S. Krøyer, FS56,
text by L. C. Nielsen (1909). fp 4 December 1909

Cantata for the Centenary of the Chamber of
Commerce, FS86, text by V. Rørdam (1917).
fp 23 April 1917

*Fynsk foraar* ('Springtime on Fyn'), Op. 42, FS96, text
by A. Berntsen (1921). fp Odense, 8 July 1922

*Hyldest til Holberg* ('Homage to Holberg'), FS102, text
by H. H. Seedorff Pedersen (1922).
fp 26 September 1922

Cantata for the Centenary of the Polytechnic High
School, FS140, text by H. H. Seedorff Pedersen (1929).
fp 30 August 1929

*Hymn to Art*, FS141, text by S. Michaelis (1929).
fp 12 October 1929

Cantata for the 50th Anniversary of the Danish
Cremation Society (*Ligbrændings-Kantate*), FS149, text
by S. Michaelis (1930). fp 30 March 1930

Cantata for the 50th Anniversary of the Young
Merchants' Education Association, FS153, text by
H. H. Seedorff Pedersen (1930). fp 3 November 1930

Cantata for the Opening of the Swimming Baths, no
FS, text by H. H. Seedorff Pedersen (1930)

## Works for Unaccompanied Choir

*Sidskensang* ('Song of the Siskin'), FS40, text by E.
Aarestrup (1906). fp 7 April 1907

*Kom Gudsengel, stille død!* ('Come Angel of God,
Tranquil Death!'), FS41, text by E. Aarestrup (1907).
fp 30 November 1907

*Aftenstemning* ('Evening Mood'), FS48, text by M.
Claudius, translated by C. Hauch (1908).
fp 19 October 1908

*Paaske-liljen* ('The Daffodil'), FS59, text by N. F. S.
Grundtvig (1910)

*Der er et yndigt land* ('There is a Lovely Land'), FS110,
text by A. Oehlenschläger (1924). fp 1 June 1924

Two School Songs (To Skolesange); *Blomsterstøv fra
Blomsterbæger* ('Pollen from the Calyx'), *Nu er for
stakket tid forbi* ('Now for a Brief Time It's Over'), texts
by V. Stuckenberg, FS138 (1929).

Three Motets (Tre Motteter): *Afflictus sum* (Psalm 38:9,
Danish and French Psalm 37)*; Dominus regit me* (Psalm
23:1-2, Danish and French Psalm 22); *Benedictus
Dominus* (Psalm 31:22, Danish and French Psalm 30),
Op. 55, FS139, texts selected by Carl Nielsen and Anne
Marie Carl-Nielsen (1929). fp 11 April 1930

*Til min fødeø* ('To the Isle of My Birth'), FS144, text by
S. P. Raben-Korch (1929)

Six Canons (For Use in Schools and Training Colleges),
FS152. 1. *Bokserne* ('The Boxers'); 2. *Traaden brister*
('The Thread Snaps'); 3. *Vægter, jeg beder* ('Watchman, I
Beg You'); 4. *Ikke det Altid slaar til* ('It isn't Always So');
5. *Du skal le ad ødelæggelse* ('At Destruction and Famine
Thou Shalt Laugh'); 6. *Stilhed og mørke* ('Silence and
Dark'), texts by 1. Carl Nielsen 2. H. C. Andersen
3. & 4. Holberg (translated by S. Müller) 5. Book of Job
6. Carl Nielsen (his motto to *Helios*) (1930).

**Vocal**

Six Songs, FS3 (miscellaneous), texts by E. Aarestrup, J. S. Welhaven, G. B. Byron, P. B. Shelley, J. J. Callanan, R. Burns; translations by 'Caralis' (C. Preetzman) (1887)

Five Songs (Fem digte af J.P. Jacobsen), Op. 4, FS12: 1. *Solnedgang* ('Sunset'); 2. *I serraillets have* ('In the Seraglio Garden'); 3. *Til Asali* ('To Asali'); 4. *Irmelin Rose*; 5. *Har dagen sænket al sin sorg* ('Has the Day Gathered All its Sorrow'), texts by J. P. Jacobsen (1891). fp 28 April 1892 (except *Til Asali*)

Songs and Verses (Viser og vers), Op. 6, FS14: 1. *Genrebillede* ('Genre Piece'); 2. *Seraferne* ('The Seraphs'); 3. *Silkesko over gylden læst* ('Silken Shoes on a Golden Last'); 4. *Det bødes der for* ('A Moment of Pleasure, an Age of Pain)'; 5. *Vise af 'Mogens'* ('Song from 'Mogens''), texts by J. P. Jacobsen (1891). fp 28 April 1892

Six Songs, Op. 10, FS18: 1. *Æbleblomst* ('Apple Blossom'); 2. *Erindringens sø* ('Lake of Memories'); 3. *Sommersang* ('Summer Song'); 4. *Sang bag ploven* ('Song Behind the Plough'); 5. *I aften* ('This Evening'); 6. *Hilsen* ('Greetings'), texts by L. Holstein (1894). fp 3 February 1898

*Du danske mand* ('Thou Danish Man'), FS35, text by H. Drachmann (1906). fp 26 June 1906

Strophic Songs, Op. 21, FS42. Vol. I: 1. *Skal blomsterne da visne* ('Shall, then, the Flowers Wither?'); 2. *Høgen* ('The Hawk'); 3. *Jens Vejmand* ('Jens the Roadmender'). Texts by: 1. H. Rode; 2. & 3. J. Aakjær. Vol. II: 1. *Sænk kun dit hoved, du blomst* ('Just Bow Your Head, Oh Flower'); 2. *Den første lærke* ('The First Lark') 3. *Husvild* ('Homeless'); 4. *Godnat* ('Goodnight'). Texts by 1. J. Jørgensen; 2. J. Aakjær; 3. & 4. J. V. Jensen (1902–7). fp 30 November 1907

*De unges sang*, ('The Young Person's Song'), FS52, text by C. Hostrup (1909)

Twenty Danish Songs (En snes dansk viser): Vol. I 1913–15 (FS70); Vol. II 1914–17 (FS78), collaboration with T. Laub. fp 13 April 1915 and 1 February 1916

*Ariel's Song*, FS80, text by Helge Rode (1916)

*Studie efter naturen* ('Study from Nature'), FS82, text by H. C. Andersen (1916)

Hymns and Sacred Songs (Salmer og aandelige Sange), FS83, 49 texts by N. F. S. Grundtvig and others, see FS Catalogue (1913–14)

*Blomstervise* ('Flower Song'), FS84, text by L. Holstein (1917)

Twenty Popular Melodies (Tyve folkelige melodier), FS95, texts by various writers, see FS Catalogue (1917–21)

Four Popular Melodies (Fire folkelige melodier), FS101: 1. *Lær mig, nattens stjerne* ('Teach Me, Oh Stars of the Night'); 2. *Sangen har lysning* ('The Song Casts Light'); 3. *Hvad synger du om?* ('Of What do You Sing?'); 4. *Nu skal det aanbares* ('Now Shall it be Revealed'), texts by 1. C. Richardt, 2. B. Björnson, 3. C. Hostrup, 4. N. F. S. Grundtvig (1922)

*Dansk arbejde* ('Danish Labour'), FS105, text by V. Rørdam (1923)

*Himlen mørkner stor og stum* ('Heaven Darkens, Great and Silent'), FS106, text by M. Falck; *Kom jul til jord* ('Come Yule to Earth'), FS107, text by J. Wiberg; *Hjemlige jule* ('Christmas at Home'), FS108, text by E. Bønnelycke (1923)

*Balladen om bjørnen* ('Ballad of the Bear'), Op. 47, FS109, text by A. Berntsen after the Swedish poet C. J. L. Almquist (1923). fp 13 March 1924

A Danish Songbook for School and Home ('Sangbogen Danmark'), by Carl Nielsen and Hakon Andersen (collection with Foreword and songs by Nielsen), FS111

Ten Little Danish Songs ('Ti danske smaasange'), FS114: 1. *Jeg ved en laerkerede* ('I Know a Lark's Nest'); 2. *Solen er saa rød mor* ('The Sun is so Red, Mother'); 3. *Tyst som aa in engen rinder* ('As Quietly as the Stream Runs in the Meadow'); 4. *Spurven sidder stum bag kvist* ('The Sparrow Sits in Silence Behind the Gable'); 5. *Den spillemand spiller paa strenge* ('The Musician is Playing his Fiddle'); 6. *Naar smaabørn klynker ved Aftentide* ('When Small Children Whimper at Eventide'); 7. *Grøn er vaarens hæk* ('Green is the Hedge in Spring'); 8. *Jeg lægger mig ass trygt til ro* ('I Settle Down to Sleep so Snugly'); 9. *O, hvor jeg er glad i dag!* ('Oh, Today I am so Happy'); 10. *Den danske sang* ('The Danish Song'), texts by various (1923–4)

Four Jutland Songs (Fire Jydske sange), FS115: 1. *Jens Madsen aa An-Sofi* ('Jens Madsen to An-Sofi'); 2. *Wo dætter* ('Our Daughter'); 3. *Den jenn aa den anden* ('One and the Other'); 4. *Æ lastræ* ('The Haypole'), texts by A. Berntsen (1924–5)

New Melodies for Johan Borup's Danish Song Book (Nye Melodier til Borups Sanbog II), FS120, texts by various (1926)

*Vocalise-etude*, for soprano and piano, FS124 (1927)

*Det är höst* ('It is Autumn'), FS121, text by A. Rogber (1929)

*Gulfloden* ('The Golden River'), FS127, text by B. S. Ingemann (1927)

*Velkommen, Lærkelil* ('Welcome, Little Lark'), FS133, text by C. Richardt (1928)

*Hjemstavn* ('My Native Soil'), FS142, text by F. Poulsen (1929)

*Fremtidensland* ('The Land of the Future'), FS145, text by B. Bjørnson (1929)

*Danmark, nu blunder den lyse nat* ('Denmark, Now Sleeps the Light Night'), FS146, text by T. Larsen (1929)

*Vi Jyde* ('We Jutlanders'), FS147, text by Bartrumsen (1929)

*Gensyn* ('Reunion'), FS151, text by Paludan-Müller (1930)

## Chamber

String Quartet in D minor, FS3d (1882–3)

Piano Trio in G major, FS3i (1883)

String Quartet in F major, FS3k (1887). fp 25 January 1888

String Quartet No. 1, in G minor, Op. 13, FS4 (1887–88, revised 1900). fp 3 February 1898

String Quintet in G major, FS5 (1888). fp 28 April 1889

String Quartet No. 2, in F minor, Op. 5, FS11 (1890). fp 8 April 1892

String Quartet No. 3, in E flat major, Op. 14, FS23 (1897–8). fp 4 October 1901

String Quartet No. 4, in F major, Op. 44, FS36, 'Piacevolezza', Op. 19 (1906, revised 1919). fp 30 November 1907

*Ved en ung kunstners baare* ('At the Bier of a Young Artist'), Andante Lamentoso, FS58, for string quintet, also arranged for string orchestra (1910). fp (funeral of Oluf Hartmann) January 1910

*Serenata in Vano*, for clarinet, bassoon, horn, cello and double bass, FS68 (1914). fp 13 April 1915

Wind Quintet, Op. 43, FS100 (1922). fp 9 October 1922

**Instrumental**

Fantasy Pieces for Piano and Clarinet in G minor, FS3h (1881?)

Sonata 'No. 1' for Violin and Piano, in G major, FS3b (1881–2)

Duet in A major, for two violins, FS3e (1882–3)

Sonata for Violin and Piano in A major, Op. 9, FS20 (1895). fp 15 January 1896

Sonata No. 2 for Violin and Piano, Op. 35, FS64 (1912). fp 7 April 1913

Three pieces for langeleg (Danish folk instrument) (1918)

*Prelude and Theme with Variations*, for solo violin, Op. 48, FS104 (1923). fp London, 28 June 1923

*Preludio e Presto*, for solo violin, Op. 52, FS128 (1927–8). fp 14 April 1928

*Canto serioso*, for horn and piano, FS132 (1913)

Allegretto for Two Recorders, FS157 (1931)

**Piano**

*Caraktærstykker* ('2 Character Pieces') for Piano, FS3f (1882–83)

Five Piano Pieces, Op. 3, FS10, 1. Folk-tune, 2. Humoresque, 3. Arabesque, 4. Mignon, 5. Elf-Dance (1890)

*Symphonic Suite*, Op. 8, FS19 (1894). fp 5 May 1895

*Humoreske-Bagateller*, Op. 11, FS22 (1894–7). fp 3 February 1898

Festival Prelude, FS24 (1899). fp 4 March 1901

*Drømmen om 'Glade Jul'* ('The Dream of a Merry Christmas'), FS34 (1905)

Chaconne, Op. 32, FS79 (1916). fp 13 April 1917

Theme with Variations, Op. 40, FS81 (1916–17). fp 29 November 1917

Piano Suite, originally called 'The Lucifer', Op. 45, FS91 (1919–20). fp 14 March 1921

Three Pieces, Op. 59, FS131 (1928). fp (first two pieces) 14 April 1928; (third piece completed) 6 November 1928

*Klavermusik for smaa og store* ('Piano Music for Young and Old', literally 'small and big'), 2 Vols., Op. 53, FS148 (1930)

Piano Piece in C, FS159 (1931)

**Organ**

29 small preludes, Op. 51, FS136; two additional preludes, FS137 (1929, 1930). fp 23 January 1930 (except 28); 19 March 1930 (complete)

*Commotio*, Op. 58, FS155 (1931). fp 14 August 1931

# Further Reading

For a full bibliography readers should consult Mina Miller's *Carl Nielsen: A Guide to Research* (New York and London, Garland Publishing, 1987). More than 400 entries straddle nine European languages, and cover everything from articles to full-length books. The full catalogue of Nielsen's musical works and some of his writings are Fog and Schousboe's *Carl Nielsen Kompositioner: en Bibliografi* (Copenhagen, NNF/Arnold Busck, 1965); its items constitute the universal FS numbers which identify Nielsen's compositions.

The bilingual catalogue of Nielsen's musical manuscripts held in the Carl Nielsen Archive in Copenhagen's Royal Library is *Carl Nielsens Samling/The Carl Nielsen Collection* (Museum Tusculanum Press at the University of Copenhagen, 1992). The musical and academic world awaits a catalogue of the composer's informal writings: journals, notes, correspondence, etc. *A Carl Nielsen Discography*, a catalogue of all recordings released in Denmark, Britain and America from 1909 to 1996, was compiled by Jack Lawson (Glasgow, The Carl Nielsen Society, 2nd ed. 1997); organized in three sections, Shellac, LP, and CD, its last section is open for regular updating.

## Writings by Carl Nielsen

*Levende musik* (Copenhagen, Martins Forlag, 1925); translated as *Living Music* by R. Spink (London, Chester Music, 1953)
This collection of short essays was gathered together on the occasion of Nielsen's sixtieth birthday.

*Min fynske barndom* (Copenhagen, Martins Forlag, 1927); translated as *My Rural Childhood* by R. Spink (London, Chester Music, 1953; Carl Nielsen Society, Glasgow, 1991)

*Breve fra Carl Nielsen til Emil B. Sachs* ('Letters from Carl Nielsen to Emil B. Sachs') (Copenhagen, Skandinavisk Grammophon Aktieselskab, 1953)

**Møller, I. E. and Meyer, T.** (eds.) *Carl Nielsens Breve i Udvalg og med Kommentatarer* (Carl Nielsen's Edited Letters with Commentaries') (Copenhagen, Gyldendal, 1954)
369 letters have been heavily edited by the composer's elder daughter Irmelin Eggert-Møller and his first biographer, Torben Meyer. A selection appeared in the Faber *Companion* (see below) in English, and the entire selection has been translated but not yet published.

**Schousboe, T.** (ed.) *Carl Nielsen Dagbøger og Brevveksling med Anne Marie Carl-Nielsen* ('Carl Nielsen's Diaries and Correspondence with Anne Marie Carl-Nielsen'), 2 Vols. (Copenhagen, Gyldendal, 1983)
Nielsen's diaries and correspondence with his wife, compiled with Irmelin's assistance until her death in 1974, have been fully annotated by Torben Schousboe. The material is edited on her instructions, especially where the breakdown of her parents' marriage is concerned.

## Primary Source Biographies and Memoirs

**Meyer, T.** (with musical analysis by F. Schandorf Petersen) *Carl Nielsen kunsteren og mennesket* ('Carl Nielsen the Artist and the Man'), 2 Vols. (Copenhagen, NNF/Arnold Busck, 1948)
Despite occasional inaccuracies, this provides important biographical data. The text is most widely circulated in its English summary as an appendix to R. Simpson's study (see below).

**Dolleris, L.** *Carl Nielsen: en musikografi* ('Carl Nielsen: A Musical Biography') (Odense, Forlag-Viggo Madsen, 1949)
A highly reverential full-length study by one of Nielsen's students

**Telmányi, A. M.** *Mit barndomshjem* ('My Childhood Home') (Copenhagen, Thaning & Appel, 1965)

**Telmányi, E.** *Af en musikers billebog* ('From a Musician's Notebook') (Copenhagen, NNF/Arnold Busck, 1978)

**Jensen, J. I.** *Carl Nielsen – danskeren* ('Carl Nielsen – the Dane') (Copenhagen, Gyldendal, 1991)
The embargo on the biographical materials contributed to a long interval before Jensen's long-awaited work, a specialized discussion of Carl Nielsen within the context of Danish culture.

## Secondary Source Biographies

**Fabricius, J.** *Carl Nielsen: A Pictorial Biography* (Copenhagen, 1965, Berlingske Forlag)
Bilingual Danish–English, highly illustrated overview

**Schousboe, T.** 'Carl Nielsen' in S. Sadie (ed.) *The New Grove Dictionary of Music and Musicians* (London, Macmillan, 1980)
Masterly biographical summary with a list of works and bibliography

**Caron, J. -L.** *Carl Nielsen: Vie et Œuvre* (Lausanne, Editions l'Age d'Homme, 1990)
Comprehensive French-language biography and reference book

**Mogensen, M. R.** *Carl Nielsen: Biographischer Dokumentationsbericht*
Comprehensive illustrated biography in 5 Vols. (Arbon, Switzerland, Verlag Eurotext Arbon [Mogensen], 1992, publication withdrawn following copyright dispute)

## Musical Analysis and Specialist Studies

**Balzer, J.** *Carl Nielsen: Centenary Essays* (Copenhagen, NNF/Arnold Busck, 1965)
There are both Danish and English editions; the latter are available from the Danish Cultural Institute, Edinburgh.

**Fanning, D. J.,** 'Carl Nielsen' in S. Sadie (ed.) *The New Grove Dictionary of Opera* (London, Macmillan, 1992)

**Fanning, D. J.** *Carl Nielsen's Fifth Symphony* (Cambridge, Cambridge University Press, forthcoming)

**Harewood, G. L. (The Earl of)** in *Kobbé's Complete Opera Book* (London, The Bodley Head, 10th edition, 1987)

**Ketting, K.** *Danish Music After Carl Nielsen* (Copenhagen, Royal Danish Ministry of Foreign Affairs, 1990)

**Miller, M. F.** (ed.) *A Carl Nielsen Companion* (London, Faber & Faber, 1994)

**Simpson, R.** *Carl Nielsen: Symphonist* (London, Dent, 1952; revised edition, London, Kahn & Averill, New York, Taplinger, 1979)

# Selective Discography

It was said during Nielsen's lifetime that he was the
best conductor of his own symphonies, and although his
songs were recorded as early as 1909, he accused the radio
of stripping music of its essential nourishment and
disparaged the gramophone's 'crackling' which impaired
the sound. This is perhaps one reason – despite the
activities of Danish Radio and the precur-sors of British
EMI and Decca – why no available recordings preserve
Nielsen's ideas of how his music should be performed.
Closest to achieving this are live concert performances by
the Danish Radio Symphony Orchestra under three
conductors who were Nielsen's colleagues: Launy
Grøndahl, Thomas Jensen, who  played in the Tivoli
Orchestra under Nielsen's baton, and who had a good
memory of Nielsen's tempos, and Erik Tuxen, whose
legendary performance of the Fifth Symphony at the
Edinburgh Festival was taped on 29 August 1950. The
Danacord label issues these and other recordings in its
valuable series, *The Historic Carl Nielsen Collection*. A
total of seventeen discs issued in six volumes includes
music of all genres and many first recordings.

Decca and His Master's Voice were active in
Denmark, and their successors' archives boast musical
treasures including the renowned Danish tenor Aksel
Schiøtz's performance of eleven of Nielsen's songs.
Many important documentary recordings were made
by Radio Denmark. Nielsen's piano music was
recorded, and in 1968 won the Gramex prize for Fona,
an independent Danish label, performed by the Danish
virtuoso, Arne Skjold Rasmussen. As yet, Fona's
successors, EMI, have not even confirmed possession of
these documentary tapes.

Probably the most desirable single 'historical reissue'
is from an independent label – Clarinet Classics couples
the renowned recording of the Clarinet Concerto
played by Louis Cahuzac with the Wind Quintet
played by the Royal Chapel Wind Quintet (as they
were called in 1936) – the very musicians who inspired
Nielsen's most popular chamber work.

Advancing some years from historical to collectable
recordings, classic examples from the 1960s – marking
the centenary of Nielsen's birth – include Stokowski's
searing performance of the Second Symphony (cur-
rently out of print) and Bernstein's of the Fifth. Both
conductors understood the life-giving properties of
music as Nielsen perceived them; each held individual
views, but were united with the composer in conceiv-
ing music to be something more than a mechanical
exercise, a diversion or mere entertainment.

Today there are many fine modern recordings of the
symphonies, but Nielsen's music continues to fall prey to
many uncommitted and unidiomatic performances.
Even world-class orchestras often fail to capture Nielsen's
essence. Newcomers to his work may find it helpful to
listen to one of the modern premium couplings, or sets,
of the symphonies. Decca's cycle with Herbert Blomstedt
and the San Francisco Symphony is consistent in artistic
and sonic qualities. Gennady Rozhdestvensky is the
third, and arguably the most successful, conductor who
has recorded the symphonies for Chandos.

The budget label Naxos can be recommended for
its CD of the Wind Quintet with a symphonic cycle on
three discs, then the piano music played by
Peter Seivewright. Second-hand record shops are an
interesting source of Nielsen recordings, Accord's
Antiquarian shop in Copenhagen being among
the best.

Where to begin can be something of a problem.
The symphonies form the safe answer, as they provide
milestones against which Nielsen's musical development
can be easily charted. But a surprise bestseller was a CD
of the complete music from *Aladdin*; it is not however
a characteristic work, and so not a true introduction to
Nielsen's music. The Fourth and Fifth Symphonies
remain his most popular works, so they are perhaps the
best introduction.

## Operas/Music for Theatre

*Aladdin*
Mette Ejsing (alto), Guido Paevatalu (baritone), Danish
Radio Symphony Orchestra conducted by Gennady
Rozhdestvensky
Chandos CHAN9135

*Maskarade*
Danish Radio Symphony Orchestra and Choir
conducted by John Frandsen
Unicorn-Kanchana DKCD9073-4 (2 CDs)

*Maskarade*
Danish Radio Symphony Orchestra conducted by Ulf
Schirmer
Decca (forthcoming)

*Saul og David* (in Danish)
Various soloists, Danish Radio Symphony Orchestra
and Choir conducted by Neeme Järvi
Chandos CHAN8911-12 (2 CDs)

*Incidental Dramatic Music*
Ole Hedegaard (tenor), Ib Nielsen (flute), Benedikte
Johansen (harp), various choirs, South Jutland
Symphony Orchestra conducted by John Frandsen
Paula PACD18

**Orchestral**

*Symphonies Nos. 1–6*
*Flute Concerto*
*Clarinet Concerto*
*Overture and Prelude to Act II of Maskarade*
*Helios*
*Pan og Syrinx*
*Rhapsodic Overture*
Julius Baker (flute), Stanley Drucker (clarinet), New
York Philharmonic Orchestra (but Symphony No. 3,
Royal Danish Orchestra) conducted by Leonard
Bernstein; Symphonies Nos. 1 and 6, and other
orchestral music, performed by the Philadelphia
Orchestra conducted by Eugene Ormandy
Sony Classics SM4K-45-989 (4 CDs)

*Symphonies Nos. 1–6*
Royal Scottish National Orchestra conducted by
Bryden Thomson
Chandos CHAN 9163-5 (3 CDs), also available singly:
1 and 2 (CHAN 8880), 3 and 5 (CHAN 9067), 4 and 6
(CHAN 9047)

*Symphonies Nos. 1–6*
San Francisco Symphony Orchestra conducted by
Herbert Blomstedt
Decca 443 117-2 (3 CDs), also available singly: 1 and 6
(425 607-2), 2 and 3 (430 280-2), 4 & 5 (421 524-2)
*Symphonies Nos. 1–6*

Royal Stockholm Philharmonic Orchestra conducted
by Gennady Rozhdestvensky
Chandos CHAN 9260, Symphonies 1 and 4 ; CHAN
9300, Symphonies 2 and 3; CHAN 9367, Symphonies 5
and 6

*Symphonies Nos. 1–6*
National Symphony Orchestra of Ireland conducted by
Adrian Leaper
Naxos 8.550743, Symphonies 4 and 5; 8.550825,
Symphonies 2 and 3; 8.550826, Symphonies 1 and 6

*Symphonies Nos. 1–6*
Danish Radio Symphony Orchestra conducted by
Launy Grøndahl (No. 2), Thomas Jensen (3, 4 and 6)
and Erik Tuxen (1 and 5)
Danacord DACO351-53 (3 CDs)

*Symphony No. 3*
*Overture to Maskarade*
*Clarinet Concerto*
Olle Schill (clarinet), Göteborg Symphony Orchestra
conducted by Myung-Whun Chung
BIS CD 321

*Symphony No. 4*
*Helios*
Swedish Radio Symphony Orchestra conducted by Esa-
Pekka Salonen
CBS MK 42093

*Symphony No. 4*
*Symphony No. 5*
*Overture to Maskarade*
BBC Symphony Orchestra conducted by Andrew Davis
Virgin Classics VC791210-2

*Aladdin* (orchestral suite)
*Overture to Maskarade*
San Francisco Symphony conducted by Herbert
Blomstedt; with Grieg's Peer Gynt Suites Nos. 1 and 2
DECCA 425-857

*Symphony No. 2*
*Aladdin* (orchestral suite)
Göteborg Symphony Orchestra conducted by Myung-
Whun Chung
BIS CD247

*Symphony No. 2*
*Pan og Syrinx*
*Aladdin* (orchestral suite)
Swedish Radio Symphony Orchestra conducted by Esa-
Pekka Salonen
SONY CLASSICS MK44934

*Violin Concerto*
*Flute Concerto*
*Clarinet Concerto*
Kim Sjøgren (violin), Toke Lund Christiansen (flute),
Niels Thomsen (clarinet), Danish Radio Symphony
Orchestra conducted by Michael Schønwandt
CHANDOS CHAN 8894

*Violin Concerto*
*Flute Concerto*
*Clarinet Concerto*
Dong-Suk Kang, (violin), Patrick Gallois (flute), Olle
Schill (clarinet), Göteborg Symphony Orchestra
conducted by Myung-Whun Chung
BIS CD616

*Violin Concerto*
Cho-Liang Lin (violin), Swedish Radio Symphony
Orchestra conducted by Esa-Pekka Salonen; with
Sibelius's Violin Concerto
SONY CLASSICS MK44548

*Violin Concerto*
*Symphony No. 4*
Arve Tellefsen (violin), Royal Philharmonic Orchestra
conducted by Yehudi Menuhin
VIRGIN CLASSICS VC-7-91111 or NORSK IDCD-5

*Flute Concerto*
Noam Buchman (flute), Oradea Philharmonic
Orchestra conducted by Erwin Acél
OLYMPIA OCD420

*Flute Concerto*
Michael Faust (flute), Cologne Radio Symphony
Orchestra conducted by Ulf Schirmer
DECCA (forthcoming)

*Clarinet Concerto*
*Little Suite for Strings*
*Pan and Syrinx*
*Overture from Amor og digteren*
Walter Boeykeus (clarinet), Beethoven Academy
conducted by Jan Caeyers
HARMONIA MUNDI HMC901489

*Clarinet Concerto*
*Wind Quintet*
*Serenata in Vano*
Louis Cahuzac (clarinet) with the Copenhagen Opera
Orchestra conducted by John Frandsen; Royal Chapel
Wind Quintet (Aage Oxenvad, clarinet, Knud Larsson,
bassoon, Hans Sorensen, horn, Louis Jensen, cello,
Louis Hegner, bass)
CLARINET CLASSICS CD CC0002

*Symphony No. 1*
*Little Suite for Strings*
New Stockholm Chamber Orchestra conducted by Esa-
Pekka Salonen
SONY CLASSICS MK42311

*Helios*
*Symphonic Rhapsody*
*Saga-drøm*
*A Fantasy Journey to the Faroes*
*Pan og Syrinx*
Danish Radio Symphony Orchestra conducted by
Gennady Rozhdestvensky
CHANDOS CHAN 9287

## Choral Works

*Hymnus amoris*
*The Sleep*
*Springtime on Fyn*
*Three Motets*
Various soloists, Danish Radio Choir conducted by
Stefan Parkman and Symphony Orchestra conducted
by Leif Segerstam (*Hymnus amoris*, The Copenhagen
Boys Choir; *Springtime on Fyn*, The Childrens Chorus
of Skt. Annæ Gymnasium)
CHANDOS CHAN8853

*Complete Works for Unaccompanied Choir*
Canzone Choir conducted by Frans Rasmussen
DANACORD DACOCD368

## Vocal

*Songs by Carl Nielsen* (157 songs)
Lars Thodberg Bertelsen (baritone), Mette Ejsing (alto),
John Laursen (tenor), Elisabeth Rehling (soprano),
Peder Severin (tenor), Eva Hess Thaysen (soprano),
Dorte Kirkesov and Tove Lønskov (piano), Jørgen Ernst
Hansen and Frode Stengaard (organ)
RONDO RCD- 8319, 8323, 8325, 8327, 8329 (5 CDs,
available singly)

*Songs*
Jørgen Klint (bass), Rosalind Bevan (piano)
PAULA PACD 56

*Songs*
Aksel Schiøtz (tenor); ten songs by C. E. F. Weyse
EMI 7-54399

*25 Hymns and Sacred Songs*
Lars Thodberg Bertelsen (baritone), Frode Stengaard
(organ); with seven preludes for organ
RONDO RCD8335

## Chamber

*String Quartets 1–4*
*String Quintet*
*Andante Lamentoso*
Kontra Quartet, Philipp Nagele (second viola), Jan
Johanson (double bass)
BIS CD503-04 (2 CDs)

*String Quartets 1–4*
*String Quintet*
*Five Movements* (unpublished: FS3c)
The Danish Quartet
KONTRAPUNKT 32150-51

*Wind Quintet*
*Serenata*
*Canto Serioso*
Athena Ensemble; with three pieces from
*The Mother*, etc.
CHANDOS CHAN8680

*Wind Quintet*
Aulos Wind Quintet; with works by Holst, Jolivet,
Pierné and Zemlinsky
KOCH SCHWANN CD310-100

*Wind Quintet*
Oslo Wind Ensemble; with wind quintets by twentieth-
century Scandinavian composers
NAXOS 8.553050

*Sonata for Violin and Piano, Op. 9*
*Sonata for Violin and Piano, Op. 35*
Kim Sjögren (violin), Anne Øland (piano)
DANACORD DACO221

*Sonata for Violin and Piano, Op. 9*
*Sonata for Violin and Piano, Op. 35*
Lydia Mordkovitch (violin), Clifford Benson (piano)
CHANDOS CHAN8598

**Piano**

*Five Piano Pieces*
*Symphonic Suite*
*Humoreske-Bagateller*
*Chaconne*
*Theme with Variations*
*The Dream of a Merry Christmas*
Peter Seivewright (piano)
Naxos 8.553574

*Festival Prelude*
*Suite*
*Three Piano Pieces*
*Piano Music for Young and Old*
Peter Seivewright (piano)
Naxos 8.553653

**Organ**

*29 Small Preludes*
*Commotio*
Ulrik Spang-Hanssen
Paula PACD 55

# Index

Page numbers in italics refer to picture captions.

**Photographic
Acknowledgements**

Edition Wilhelm Hansen,
    Copenhagen: 83, 89
The Hulton Getty Picture
    Collection Ltd, London: 37,
    41r, 64, 73, 177
Det Kongelige Bibliotek,
    Copenhagen: 13, 15, 18, 23, 27,
    29, 33, 34, 35, 42, 44, 49, 57,
    60–1, 87, 92–3, 97, 100–1,
    104, 109, 118, 122–3, 124,
    126–7, 128, 130, 132–3, 139, 141,
    142, 143, 145, 150, 152, 156–7,
    161, 163, 164, 168, 172, 174, 181,
    184, 186, 195, 197, 204, 209, 211
The Lebrecht Collection, London:
    41l, 46–7, 54, 76–7, 85, 207
Det Nationalhistoriske Museum
    paa Frederiksborg, Hillerod:
    38–9
Odense Bys Museer/Carl Nielsen
    Museet, Odense: 70–1, 80,
    148, 170–1, 178–9, 199, 201,
    217
Photo Phil Cutts/Opera North,
    Leeds: 110–11
Polfoto, Copenhagen: 2, 24–5, 63,
    113, 214–15, 216
Photo E. H. Thorning/Private
    Collection: 116–17